50 French Dessert Recipes for Home

By: Kelly Johnson

Table of Contents

- Crème Brûlée
- Tarte Tatin
- Éclairs
- Macarons
- Clafoutis
- Profiteroles
- Mille-Feuille
- Madeleines
- Mousse au Chocolat
- Galette des Rois
- Canelés
- Paris-Brest
- Baba au Rhum
- Financiers
- Soufflé
- Tarte aux Fraises
- Pâte de Fruits
- Croquembouche
- Tarte au Citron
- Gâteau Basque
- Chouquettes
- Pain d'Épices
- Far Breton
- Crêpes Suzette
- Chaussons aux Pommes
- Tarte Tropézienne
- Île Flottante
- Quatre-Quarts
- Kouign-Amann
- Gâteau Opéra
- Bûche de Noël
- Pithiviers
- Gâteau Saint-Honoré
- Poire Belle Hélène
- Palmier

- Sablés
- Tarte Normande
- Beignets
- Mont Blanc
- Religieuse
- Tarte Bourdaloue
- Gâteau Moelleux au Chocolat
- Riz au Lait
- Flan Parisien
- Tarte aux Abricots
- Petits Pots de Crème
- Navettes Provençales
- Pain Perdu
- Charlotte aux Fraises
- Croissant Bread Pudding

Crème Brûlée

Ingredients:

- 1 quart (950ml) heavy cream
- 1 vanilla bean or 1 tablespoon vanilla extract
- 6 large egg yolks
- 3/4 cup (150g) granulated sugar, plus extra for caramelizing

Instructions:

1. Preheat oven: Preheat your oven to 325°F (160°C). Place 6 to 8 ramekins (depending on their size) in a baking dish or roasting pan. Set aside.
2. Prepare vanilla-infused cream: In a saucepan, heat the heavy cream over medium heat until it just starts to simmer. If using a vanilla bean, split it lengthwise and scrape the seeds into the cream. Add the vanilla bean pod (if using) to the cream. Remove from heat and let it steep for about 10-15 minutes to infuse the cream with vanilla flavor. If using vanilla extract, stir it into the cream after it has been heated.
3. Prepare custard: In a mixing bowl, whisk together the egg yolks and granulated sugar until well combined and slightly pale in color. Gradually pour the hot cream into the egg yolk mixture, whisking constantly, to temper the eggs.
4. Strain mixture: Strain the custard mixture through a fine-mesh sieve into a clean bowl to remove any lumps or bits of vanilla bean. Discard the vanilla bean pod.
5. Fill ramekins: Divide the custard mixture evenly among the ramekins. Carefully pour hot water into the baking dish or roasting pan until it reaches about halfway up the sides of the ramekins, creating a water bath for even baking.
6. Bake: Bake the Crème Brûlée in the preheated oven for about 30-40 minutes, or until the custard is set around the edges but still slightly jiggly in the center. The cooking time may vary depending on the size of your ramekins.
7. Chill: Remove the ramekins from the water bath and let them cool to room temperature. Then, cover and refrigerate them for at least 2-3 hours, or until completely chilled and set.
8. Caramelize sugar: Just before serving, sprinkle a thin, even layer of granulated sugar over the top of each chilled Crème Brûlée. Use a kitchen torch to carefully caramelize the sugar until it forms a golden-brown crust. Alternatively, you can place the ramekins under a broiler for a few minutes until the sugar caramelizes.

9. Serve: Let the Crème Brûlée sit for a minute or two to allow the caramelized sugar to harden. Serve immediately and enjoy the contrasting textures of creamy custard and crunchy caramelized sugar.

Crème Brûlée is a decadent and elegant dessert that is sure to impress your guests. It's perfect for special occasions or anytime you want to indulge in a luxurious treat. Buon appetito!

Tarte Tatin

Ingredients:

For the pastry crust:

- 1 1/4 cups (160g) all-purpose flour
- 1/2 cup (115g) unsalted butter, cold and cubed
- 1/4 cup (50g) granulated sugar
- 1/4 teaspoon salt
- 2-3 tablespoons ice water

For the filling:

- 6-8 apples (such as Granny Smith or Gala), peeled, cored, and quartered
- 1/2 cup (100g) granulated sugar
- 1/4 cup (55g) unsalted butter, cubed
- 1 teaspoon vanilla extract
- Zest of 1 lemon (optional)
- Pinch of cinnamon (optional)

Instructions:

1. Prepare pastry crust: In a large mixing bowl, combine the all-purpose flour, granulated sugar, and salt. Add the cold, cubed butter and use your fingertips or a pastry cutter to cut the butter into the flour mixture until it resembles coarse crumbs. Gradually add the ice water, 1 tablespoon at a time, and mix until the dough comes together. Shape the dough into a disk, wrap it in plastic wrap, and refrigerate for at least 30 minutes.
2. Caramelize apples: Preheat your oven to 375°F (190°C). In a 9 or 10-inch (23-25cm) oven-safe skillet or Tatin dish, melt the unsalted butter over medium heat. Sprinkle the granulated sugar evenly over the melted butter. Arrange the apple quarters in a single layer in the skillet, rounded side down. Cook the apples, without stirring, for about 10-15 minutes, or until they start to caramelize and soften. If desired, add the vanilla extract, lemon zest, and pinch of cinnamon during this step.
3. Roll out pastry crust: Remove the chilled pastry dough from the refrigerator and roll it out on a lightly floured surface into a circle slightly larger than the skillet or Tatin dish.

4. Assemble Tarte Tatin: Carefully place the pastry dough over the caramelized apples in the skillet, tucking in any excess dough around the edges. Prick the pastry dough all over with a fork to allow steam to escape during baking.
5. Bake: Bake the Tarte Tatin in the preheated oven for about 25-30 minutes, or until the pastry is golden brown and cooked through.
6. Invert and serve: Remove the Tarte Tatin from the oven and let it cool in the skillet for a few minutes. Place a serving plate or platter over the skillet and carefully invert the Tarte Tatin onto the plate, being mindful of any hot caramel. Serve the Tarte Tatin warm or at room temperature, optionally with a dollop of whipped cream or a scoop of vanilla ice cream.

Tarte Tatin is a delicious and impressive dessert that's perfect for showcasing seasonal fruits. Its caramelized apple filling and buttery pastry crust are sure to delight your taste buds. Enjoy this classic French treat with family and friends!

Éclairs

Ingredients:

For the choux pastry:

- 1/2 cup (120ml) water
- 1/2 cup (120ml) whole milk
- 1/2 cup (115g) unsalted butter, cut into cubes
- 1 tablespoon granulated sugar
- 1/4 teaspoon salt
- 1 cup (125g) all-purpose flour
- 4 large eggs

For the pastry cream:

- 2 cups (480ml) whole milk
- 1/2 cup (100g) granulated sugar
- 4 large egg yolks
- 1/4 cup (30g) cornstarch
- 1 teaspoon vanilla extract

For the chocolate glaze:

- 1/2 cup (120ml) heavy cream
- 4 ounces (115g) semisweet chocolate, chopped
- 1 tablespoon unsalted butter

Instructions:

For the choux pastry:

1. Preheat oven: Preheat your oven to 400°F (200°C). Line a baking sheet with parchment paper or a silicone baking mat.
2. Prepare dough: In a saucepan, combine water, milk, butter, sugar, and salt. Bring to a boil over medium heat. Remove from heat and add the flour all at once. Stir vigorously with a wooden spoon until the mixture forms a ball and pulls away from the sides of the pan.
3. Add eggs: Transfer the dough to a mixing bowl. Let it cool for a few minutes. Beat in the eggs, one at a time, mixing well after each addition, until the dough is smooth and glossy.

4. Pipe dough: Transfer the dough to a pastry bag fitted with a large round tip. Pipe the dough onto the prepared baking sheet into 4-5 inch (10-12 cm) long strips, spacing them about 2 inches (5 cm) apart.
5. Bake: Bake in the preheated oven for 15 minutes. Reduce the oven temperature to 350°F (180°C) and continue to bake for another 20-25 minutes, or until the éclairs are golden brown and puffed. Remove from the oven and let them cool completely on a wire rack.

For the pastry cream:

1. Heat milk: In a saucepan, heat the milk over medium heat until it just starts to simmer.
2. Mix egg yolks: In a mixing bowl, whisk together the granulated sugar and egg yolks until pale and creamy. Add the cornstarch and whisk until smooth.
3. Temper eggs: Gradually pour the hot milk into the egg mixture, whisking constantly, to temper the eggs.
4. Cook mixture: Return the mixture to the saucepan and cook over medium heat, stirring constantly, until it thickens and comes to a boil. Remove from heat and stir in the vanilla extract.
5. Chill: Transfer the pastry cream to a clean bowl and cover the surface with plastic wrap to prevent a skin from forming. Refrigerate until chilled and set.

For the chocolate glaze:

1. Heat cream: In a saucepan, heat the heavy cream over medium heat until it just starts to simmer.
2. Melt chocolate: Place the chopped chocolate in a heatproof bowl. Pour the hot cream over the chocolate and let it sit for a minute. Stir until the chocolate is melted and smooth. Stir in the butter until melted and incorporated.

Assembly:

1. Fill éclairs: Use a small round tip or a pastry bag fitted with a round tip to make a small hole in one end of each éclair. Fill the éclairs with the chilled pastry cream.
2. Glaze éclairs: Dip the top of each éclair into the chocolate glaze, allowing any excess glaze to drip off. Place the glazed éclairs on a wire rack set over a baking sheet to catch any drips. Let the glaze set for a few minutes before serving.
3. Serve: Serve the éclairs immediately, or store them in the refrigerator until ready to serve. Enjoy this classic French pastry as a delightful treat!

Éclairs are a versatile dessert that can be customized with different fillings and glazes to suit your preferences. Whether you prefer classic vanilla pastry cream or decadent chocolate ganache, these éclairs are sure to impress!

Macarons

Ingredients:

For the macaron shells:

- 1 3/4 cups (200g) almond flour
- 1 3/4 cups (210g) powdered sugar
- 3 large egg whites, at room temperature
- 1/4 cup (50g) granulated sugar
- Gel food coloring (optional)

For the filling:

- 1/2 cup (120ml) heavy cream
- 4 ounces (115g) semisweet or bittersweet chocolate, chopped
- 2 tablespoons unsalted butter, at room temperature

Instructions:

For the macaron shells:

1. Prepare baking sheets: Line two baking sheets with parchment paper or silicone baking mats. If using parchment paper, you can trace circles onto the paper to use as a guide for piping the macarons.
2. Prepare almond mixture: In a food processor, combine the almond flour and powdered sugar. Pulse until finely ground and well combined. Sift the mixture through a fine-mesh sieve into a large mixing bowl. Discard any large pieces that remain in the sieve.
3. Whip egg whites: In a clean, dry mixing bowl, beat the egg whites with an electric mixer on medium speed until foamy. Gradually add the granulated sugar, a spoonful at a time, while continuing to beat. Increase the speed to high and beat until stiff peaks form. If using, add gel food coloring and beat until the color is evenly distributed.
4. Fold in almond mixture: Add half of the almond mixture to the whipped egg whites. Gently fold with a spatula until just combined. Add the remaining almond mixture and continue to fold until the batter is smooth and glossy, with a thick, ribbon-like consistency. Be careful not to overmix.
5. Pipe macarons: Transfer the batter to a pastry bag fitted with a round tip. Pipe small circles onto the prepared baking sheets, using the traced circles as a guide. Leave some space between each circle as the macarons will spread slightly.

6. Rest and dry: Tap the baking sheets on the counter a few times to release any air bubbles. Let the piped macarons sit at room temperature for about 30-60 minutes, or until a thin, dry film forms on the surface. This will help the macarons develop a smooth, shiny exterior during baking.
7. Preheat oven: Preheat your oven to 300°F (150°C) while the macarons are resting.
8. Bake: Bake the macarons in the preheated oven for about 15-18 minutes, or until they are set and lift easily off the parchment paper. Let them cool completely on the baking sheets before removing them.

For the filling:

1. Prepare ganache: In a small saucepan, heat the heavy cream until it just starts to simmer. Place the chopped chocolate in a heatproof bowl. Pour the hot cream over the chocolate and let it sit for a minute. Stir until the chocolate is melted and smooth. Stir in the butter until melted and incorporated. Let the ganache cool to room temperature, or until it reaches a spreadable consistency.
2. Assemble macarons: Pair up the cooled macaron shells according to size. Spread or pipe a small amount of ganache onto the flat side of one shell and sandwich it with another shell. Gently press down to secure the filling.
3. Chill and serve: Place the assembled macarons in an airtight container and refrigerate for at least 24 hours before serving. This allows the flavors to meld and the texture to develop. Serve the macarons chilled or at room temperature.

Macarons are a delightful and elegant treat that are perfect for special occasions or any time you want to indulge in something sweet. With practice and patience, you can create beautiful and delicious macarons at home!

Clafoutis

Ingredients:

- 1 tablespoon unsalted butter, for greasing the baking dish
- 1 cup (150g) fresh cherries, pitted (or other fruits such as berries, plums, or sliced peaches)
- 3 large eggs
- 1/2 cup (100g) granulated sugar
- 1 cup (240ml) whole milk
- 1/2 cup (60g) all-purpose flour
- 1 teaspoon vanilla extract
- Pinch of salt
- Powdered sugar, for dusting (optional)

Instructions:

1. Preheat oven: Preheat your oven to 350°F (180°C). Grease a 9-inch (23cm) round baking dish with unsalted butter.
2. Prepare fruit: If using cherries, pit them using a cherry pitter or a paring knife. If using other fruits, prepare them as needed (e.g., wash berries, slice peaches, etc.). Arrange the prepared fruit in an even layer in the greased baking dish.
3. Make batter: In a mixing bowl, whisk together the eggs and granulated sugar until pale and slightly thickened. Add the whole milk, all-purpose flour, vanilla extract, and a pinch of salt. Whisk until the batter is smooth and well combined.
4. Pour batter over fruit: Pour the batter evenly over the prepared fruit in the baking dish.
5. Bake: Bake the Clafoutis in the preheated oven for about 30-35 minutes, or until the top is golden brown and the center is set. The Clafoutis will puff up slightly during baking and may have a slightly jiggly center, which is normal.
6. Cool and serve: Remove the Clafoutis from the oven and let it cool slightly. Dust the top with powdered sugar, if desired. Serve the Clafoutis warm or at room temperature, either on its own or with a dollop of whipped cream or a scoop of vanilla ice cream.

Clafoutis is a delightful dessert that's perfect for showcasing seasonal fruits. Its custardy texture and subtle sweetness make it a comforting treat that's sure to please. Enjoy it as a delicious ending to a meal or as a special indulgence any time of day!

Profiteroles

Ingredients:

For the choux pastry:

- 1/2 cup (120ml) water
- 1/4 cup (60g) unsalted butter
- 1/2 cup (60g) all-purpose flour
- 2 large eggs
- Pinch of salt

For the filling:

- 1 cup (240ml) heavy cream
- 2 tablespoons powdered sugar
- 1 teaspoon vanilla extract

For the chocolate sauce (optional):

- 4 ounces (115g) semisweet or bittersweet chocolate, chopped
- 1/2 cup (120ml) heavy cream
- 2 tablespoons unsalted butter
- 1 tablespoon granulated sugar (optional)

Instructions:

For the choux pastry:

1. Preheat oven: Preheat your oven to 425°F (220°C). Line a baking sheet with parchment paper or a silicone baking mat.
2. Prepare dough: In a saucepan, combine water, butter, and salt. Bring to a boil over medium heat. Remove from heat and add the flour all at once. Stir vigorously with a wooden spoon until the mixture forms a ball and pulls away from the sides of the pan.
3. Add eggs: Transfer the dough to a mixing bowl. Let it cool for a few minutes. Beat in the eggs, one at a time, mixing well after each addition, until the dough is smooth and glossy.
4. Pipe dough: Transfer the dough to a pastry bag fitted with a large round tip. Pipe small mounds onto the prepared baking sheet, leaving space between each one for expansion.

5. Bake: Bake in the preheated oven for 15 minutes. Reduce the oven temperature to 375°F (190°C) and continue to bake for another 10-15 minutes, or until the profiteroles are golden brown and puffed. Remove from the oven and let them cool completely on a wire rack.

For the filling:

1. Whip cream: In a mixing bowl, whip the heavy cream, powdered sugar, and vanilla extract until stiff peaks form.
2. Fill profiteroles: Once the profiteroles are cool, use a serrated knife to slice them in half horizontally. Pipe or spoon the whipped cream onto the bottom halves of the profiteroles. Place the top halves back on.

For the chocolate sauce (optional):

1. Prepare chocolate sauce: In a heatproof bowl, combine the chopped chocolate, heavy cream, butter, and granulated sugar (if using). Place the bowl over a saucepan of simmering water (double boiler) and stir until the chocolate is melted and the mixture is smooth.
2. Drizzle sauce: Drizzle the chocolate sauce over the filled profiteroles or serve it on the side for dipping.

Serve:

Serve the profiteroles immediately, garnished with powdered sugar if desired. They can also be chilled in the refrigerator until ready to serve. Enjoy these delightful pastries as a decadent dessert or a special treat any time of day!

Mille-Feuille

Ingredients:

For the puff pastry:

- 1 sheet of store-bought puff pastry (or homemade if preferred)

For the pastry cream:

- 2 cups (480ml) whole milk
- 1/2 cup (100g) granulated sugar
- 4 large egg yolks
- 1/4 cup (30g) cornstarch
- 1 teaspoon vanilla extract

For assembly:

- Powdered sugar, for dusting
- Optional: fondant icing or chocolate glaze

Instructions:

For the puff pastry:

1. Preheat oven: Preheat your oven to the temperature indicated on the puff pastry package instructions (usually around 400°F or 200°C).
2. Prepare puff pastry: Roll out the puff pastry on a lightly floured surface to about 1/4 inch (6mm) thickness. Cut the pastry into three equal-sized rectangles. Place the rectangles on a baking sheet lined with parchment paper.
3. Bake: Prick the surface of each rectangle with a fork to prevent puffing too much. Bake in the preheated oven for about 15-20 minutes, or until golden brown and puffed. Remove from the oven and let cool completely on a wire rack.

For the pastry cream:

1. Heat milk: In a saucepan, heat the whole milk over medium heat until it just starts to simmer.
2. Mix egg yolks: In a mixing bowl, whisk together the granulated sugar and egg yolks until pale and creamy. Add the cornstarch and whisk until smooth.
3. Temper eggs: Gradually pour the hot milk into the egg mixture, whisking constantly, to temper the eggs.

4. Cook mixture: Return the mixture to the saucepan and cook over medium heat, stirring constantly, until it thickens and comes to a boil. Remove from heat and stir in the vanilla extract.
5. Chill: Transfer the pastry cream to a clean bowl and cover the surface with plastic wrap to prevent a skin from forming. Refrigerate until chilled and set.

Assembly:

1. Layer puff pastry and pastry cream: Place one rectangle of puff pastry on a serving platter or cake stand. Spread a layer of pastry cream evenly over the puff pastry. Place another rectangle of puff pastry on top and press down gently. Repeat with another layer of pastry cream and the remaining rectangle of puff pastry.
2. Top layer: Place the final rectangle of puff pastry on top. Dust the top with powdered sugar or spread a thin layer of fondant icing or chocolate glaze over the top, if desired.
3. Chill and serve: Refrigerate the mille-feuille for at least 1 hour before serving to allow the layers to set. Slice into portions using a sharp knife and serve chilled.

Mille-feuille is a delightful and elegant dessert that's perfect for special occasions or as a sweet treat any time of day. Its crisp, flaky layers of puff pastry and creamy pastry cream filling make it a favorite among pastry lovers. Enjoy!

Madeleines

Ingredients:

- 2/3 cup (135g) granulated sugar
- 3 large eggs, at room temperature
- 1 teaspoon vanilla extract
- 1 teaspoon lemon zest (optional)
- 1/4 teaspoon salt
- 1 cup (125g) all-purpose flour
- 1 teaspoon baking powder
- 10 tablespoons (140g) unsalted butter, melted and cooled slightly, plus extra for greasing the molds
- Powdered sugar, for dusting (optional)

Instructions:

1. Preheat oven: Preheat your oven to 375°F (190°C). Grease the madeleine molds with melted butter and dust with flour, tapping out any excess flour.
2. Beat eggs and sugar: In a mixing bowl, beat the eggs and granulated sugar together with an electric mixer on high speed until pale and thickened, about 5 minutes. The mixture should leave a ribbon-like trail when the beaters are lifted.
3. Add flavorings: Mix in the vanilla extract and lemon zest, if using, until well combined.
4. Fold in dry ingredients: In a separate bowl, sift together the all-purpose flour, baking powder, and salt. Gradually fold the dry ingredients into the egg mixture using a spatula, being careful not to deflate the batter.
5. Add melted butter: Gently fold in the melted butter until just combined.
6. Fill molds: Spoon the batter into the prepared madeleine molds, filling each mold about three-quarters full.
7. Bake: Bake in the preheated oven for 10-12 minutes, or until the madeleines are golden brown around the edges and spring back when lightly pressed.
8. Cool: Remove the madeleines from the oven and let them cool in the molds for a few minutes. Then, carefully transfer them to a wire rack to cool completely.
9. Serve: Once cooled, dust the madeleines with powdered sugar, if desired. Serve them slightly warm or at room temperature.

Madeleines are best enjoyed fresh on the day they are made, but they can be stored in an airtight container for up to 2-3 days. Enjoy these delightful little cakes as a sweet treat with your favorite hot beverage!

Mousse au Chocolat

Ingredients:

- 7 ounces (200g) bittersweet or semisweet chocolate, chopped
- 4 large eggs, separated
- 1/4 cup (50g) granulated sugar
- 1 cup (240ml) heavy cream
- 1 teaspoon vanilla extract
- Pinch of salt

Instructions:

1. Melt chocolate: Place the chopped chocolate in a heatproof bowl set over a saucepan of simmering water (double boiler). Stir occasionally until the chocolate is melted and smooth. Remove from heat and let it cool slightly.
2. Whip egg whites: In a clean, dry mixing bowl, beat the egg whites with an electric mixer on high speed until soft peaks form. Gradually add half of the granulated sugar and continue to beat until stiff peaks form. Set aside.
3. Whip cream: In another mixing bowl, whip the heavy cream, remaining granulated sugar, vanilla extract, and salt until stiff peaks form.
4. Combine egg yolks and chocolate: In a separate mixing bowl, whisk the egg yolks until smooth. Gradually whisk in the melted chocolate until well combined.
5. Fold in whipped cream: Gently fold the whipped cream into the chocolate mixture until no streaks remain.
6. Fold in egg whites: Gently fold the beaten egg whites into the chocolate mixture until well combined and no white streaks remain. Be careful not to overmix, as this will deflate the mousse.
7. Chill: Spoon the chocolate mousse into serving glasses or bowls. Cover and refrigerate for at least 2 hours, or until set.
8. Serve: Serve the chocolate mousse chilled, garnished with whipped cream, chocolate shavings, or fresh berries, if desired.

Chocolate mousse is a luxurious and elegant dessert that's perfect for special occasions or as a sweet treat any time of day. Its rich chocolate flavor and airy texture make it a delightful indulgence for chocolate lovers. Enjoy!

Galette des Rois

Ingredients:

For the puff pastry:

- 2 sheets of store-bought puff pastry (or homemade if preferred)

For the frangipane filling:

- 1 cup (100g) almond flour
- 1/2 cup (100g) granulated sugar
- 1/2 cup (115g) unsalted butter, softened
- 2 large eggs
- 1 teaspoon almond extract (or vanilla extract)
- 1 tablespoon all-purpose flour

For assembly:

- 1 egg yolk, beaten (for egg wash)
- 1 fève or small figurine (optional)

Instructions:

1. Prepare puff pastry: Preheat your oven to the temperature indicated on the puff pastry package instructions (usually around 400°F or 200°C). Roll out one sheet of puff pastry into a circle on a lightly floured surface, then transfer it to a parchment-lined baking sheet.
2. Prepare frangipane filling: In a mixing bowl, cream together the almond flour, granulated sugar, softened butter, eggs, almond extract, and all-purpose flour until smooth and well combined.
3. Spread filling: Spread the frangipane filling evenly over the center of the rolled-out puff pastry, leaving a border around the edges.
4. Place trinket: If using a fève or small figurine, gently press it into the filling, making sure it's hidden.
5. Prepare second sheet of puff pastry: Roll out the second sheet of puff pastry into a circle on a lightly floured surface. Place it over the filling, pressing down gently around the edges to seal.
6. Crimp edges: Use a fork to crimp the edges of the Galette des Rois to seal them together. You can also use your fingers to create a decorative pattern if desired.

7. Brush with egg wash: Brush the top of the Galette des Rois with beaten egg yolk to give it a golden brown color when baked.
8. Bake: Bake in the preheated oven for about 25-30 minutes, or until the Galette is golden brown and puffed.
9. Serve: Let the Galette des Rois cool slightly before serving. Traditionally, it is served at room temperature. Cut into slices and enjoy with family and friends. The person who finds the fève in their slice is crowned king or queen for the day!

Galette des Rois is a delicious and festive dessert that's perfect for celebrating the Epiphany or any special occasion. Enjoy this traditional French treat with loved ones and continue the time-honored tradition of crowning the king or queen of the day!

Canelés

Ingredients:

- 2 cups (480ml) whole milk
- 2 tablespoons unsalted butter
- 1 vanilla bean, split lengthwise (or 2 teaspoons vanilla extract)
- 1 cup (200g) granulated sugar
- 1 cup (120g) all-purpose flour
- 4 large egg yolks
- 1/4 cup (60ml) dark rum
- Butter or beeswax for greasing molds

Instructions:

1. Prepare molds: Grease the canelé molds generously with melted butter or beeswax. Place the molds on a baking sheet and refrigerate them while you prepare the batter.
2. Infuse milk: In a saucepan, heat the whole milk, unsalted butter, and split vanilla bean (scraped seeds and pod) over medium heat until it just starts to simmer. Remove from heat and let it cool slightly to infuse the flavors.
3. Make batter: In a mixing bowl, whisk together the granulated sugar and all-purpose flour. Gradually whisk in the warm milk mixture until smooth. Whisk in the egg yolks one at a time until well combined. Stir in the dark rum.
4. Chill batter: Cover the bowl with plastic wrap and refrigerate the batter for at least 24 hours, or up to 48 hours. This resting period allows the flavors to develop and the batter to thicken.
5. Preheat oven: Preheat your oven to 450°F (230°C) and place a rack in the center of the oven.
6. Fill molds: Give the batter a good stir, then fill each chilled canelé mold about three-quarters full with the batter.
7. Bake: Place the baking sheet with the filled molds in the preheated oven and bake for 15 minutes.
8. Reduce heat: Reduce the oven temperature to 375°F (190°C) and continue to bake for another 50-55 minutes, or until the canelés are dark golden brown and caramelized on the outside, and set in the center.
9. Cool: Remove the canelés from the oven and let them cool in the molds for a few minutes. Then, carefully remove them from the molds and transfer them to a wire rack to cool completely.

10. Serve: Enjoy the canelés at room temperature. They are best eaten the day they are made but can be stored in an airtight container at room temperature for up to 2 days.

Canelés are a delightful treat with a unique flavor and texture, making them a favorite among pastry lovers. Enjoy them as a sweet indulgence with a cup of coffee or tea!

Paris-Brest

Ingredients:

For the choux pastry:

- 1/2 cup (120ml) water
- 1/2 cup (120ml) whole milk
- 1/2 cup (115g) unsalted butter
- 1 tablespoon granulated sugar
- 1/4 teaspoon salt
- 1 cup (125g) all-purpose flour
- 4 large eggs

For the praline cream filling:

- 1 cup (240ml) heavy cream
- 1/4 cup (50g) granulated sugar
- 1/2 cup (60g) ground almonds
- 1/4 cup (30g) powdered sugar
- 1/2 teaspoon vanilla extract

For assembly:

- Sliced almonds or powdered sugar for topping

Instructions:

For the choux pastry:

1. Preheat oven: Preheat your oven to 425°F (220°C). Line a baking sheet with parchment paper or a silicone baking mat.
2. Prepare dough: In a saucepan, combine water, milk, butter, sugar, and salt. Bring to a boil over medium heat. Remove from heat and add the flour all at once. Stir vigorously with a wooden spoon until the mixture forms a ball and pulls away from the sides of the pan.
3. Add eggs: Transfer the dough to a mixing bowl. Let it cool for a few minutes. Beat in the eggs, one at a time, mixing well after each addition, until the dough is smooth and glossy.

4. Pipe dough: Transfer the dough to a pastry bag fitted with a large round tip. Pipe a ring onto the prepared baking sheet, about 10 inches (25cm) in diameter, leaving a hole in the center.
5. Bake: Bake in the preheated oven for 15 minutes. Reduce the oven temperature to 375°F (190°C) and continue to bake for another 20-25 minutes, or until the pastry is golden brown and puffed. Remove from the oven and let it cool completely on a wire rack.

For the praline cream filling:

1. Prepare praline: In a small saucepan, combine the ground almonds and granulated sugar over medium heat. Cook, stirring constantly, until the sugar melts and caramelizes, about 5-7 minutes. Remove from heat and let it cool slightly.
2. Whip cream: In a mixing bowl, whip the heavy cream and powdered sugar until stiff peaks form. Fold in the vanilla extract and the cooled praline mixture until well combined.

For assembly:

1. Slice pastry: Use a serrated knife to slice the cooled choux pastry in half horizontally.
2. Fill pastry: Spoon or pipe the praline cream filling onto the bottom half of the choux pastry. Place the top half of the pastry on top of the filling.
3. Top: Sprinkle sliced almonds or powdered sugar over the top of the Paris-Brest for decoration.
4. Serve: Slice and serve the Paris-Brest immediately. Enjoy this delightful French pastry as a sweet treat or dessert!

Paris-Brest is a decadent and delicious dessert that's sure to impress with its unique ring shape and flavorful praline cream filling. Enjoy it with friends and family for a special occasion or as a delightful indulgence any time!

Baba au Rhum

Ingredients:

For the baba dough:

- 2 1/4 teaspoons (1 packet) active dry yeast
- 1/4 cup (60ml) warm water (110°F/45°C)
- 2 cups (250g) all-purpose flour
- 3 large eggs, at room temperature
- 1/4 cup (50g) granulated sugar
- 1/2 teaspoon salt
- 1/2 cup (115g) unsalted butter, softened

For the rum syrup:

- 1 cup (240ml) water
- 1 cup (200g) granulated sugar
- 3/4 cup (180ml) dark rum

For serving:

- Whipped cream or pastry cream

Instructions:

For the baba dough:

1. Activate yeast: In a small bowl, dissolve the yeast in warm water and let it sit for 5-10 minutes until frothy.
2. Mix dough: In a mixing bowl, combine the flour, eggs, sugar, salt, and softened butter. Mix until well combined. Add the activated yeast mixture and continue to mix until the dough is smooth and elastic.
3. First rise: Cover the bowl with plastic wrap and let the dough rise in a warm, draft-free place for about 1-2 hours, or until doubled in size.
4. Shape dough: Grease a baba mold or muffin tin with butter. Punch down the risen dough and divide it evenly into the prepared molds. Cover loosely with plastic wrap and let it rise again for another 30-45 minutes.
5. Preheat oven: Preheat your oven to 375°F (190°C).

6. Bake: Bake the baba dough in the preheated oven for 15-20 minutes, or until golden brown and cooked through. Remove from the oven and let them cool slightly.

For the rum syrup:

1. Prepare syrup: In a saucepan, combine the water and granulated sugar. Bring to a simmer over medium heat, stirring until the sugar is dissolved. Remove from heat and stir in the dark rum.
2. Soak baba: While the baba are still warm, carefully remove them from the molds and place them in a shallow dish. Pour the rum syrup over the warm baba, ensuring they are fully soaked. Let them sit for at least 30 minutes to absorb the syrup.

For serving:

1. Serve: Serve the baba au rhum with whipped cream or pastry cream on the side.
2. Enjoy: Enjoy this decadent dessert with its rich rum flavor and moist, tender texture.

Baba au Rhum is a delightful and indulgent dessert that's sure to impress with its rich flavor and elegant presentation. Enjoy it as a sweet treat for special occasions or whenever you're in the mood for a luxurious dessert experience!

Financiers

Ingredients:

- 1/2 cup (115g) unsalted butter, plus extra for greasing the molds
- 1 cup (100g) almond flour
- 1 cup (100g) powdered sugar
- 1/2 cup (60g) all-purpose flour
- 1/4 teaspoon salt
- 4 large egg whites, at room temperature
- 1 teaspoon vanilla extract
- Optional: Sliced almonds for garnish

Instructions:

1. Preheat oven: Preheat your oven to 375°F (190°C). Grease the financier molds with melted butter or non-stick cooking spray.
2. Brown butter: In a saucepan, melt the butter over medium heat. Continue to cook, stirring occasionally, until the butter starts to brown and develop a nutty aroma, about 5-7 minutes. Remove from heat and let it cool slightly.
3. Mix dry ingredients: In a mixing bowl, whisk together the almond flour, powdered sugar, all-purpose flour, and salt until well combined.
4. Whip egg whites: In another mixing bowl, whisk the egg whites until frothy but not stiff. Gradually fold in the dry ingredients until just combined.
5. Add brown butter: Gradually pour in the cooled browned butter while continuing to mix, until the batter is smooth and well combined. Stir in the vanilla extract.
6. Fill molds: Fill the prepared financier molds about three-quarters full with the batter. If desired, sprinkle sliced almonds on top of each cake for garnish.
7. Bake: Bake in the preheated oven for 12-15 minutes, or until the financiers are golden brown around the edges and spring back lightly when touched.
8. Cool: Remove the financiers from the oven and let them cool in the molds for a few minutes. Then, transfer them to a wire rack to cool completely.
9. Serve: Serve the financiers at room temperature as a delightful sweet treat with tea or coffee.

Financiers are best enjoyed on the day they are made but can be stored in an airtight container at room temperature for up to 2 days. They're a simple yet elegant dessert that's sure to impress with their delicate almond flavor and moist texture. Enjoy!

Soufflé

Ingredients:

- 2 tablespoons unsalted butter, plus extra for greasing the soufflé dish
- 1/4 cup (30g) grated Parmesan cheese, for coating the soufflé dish
- 1/4 cup (30g) all-purpose flour
- 1 cup (240ml) whole milk
- 1 cup (100g) grated Gruyère cheese (or any other cheese of your choice)
- 4 large eggs, separated
- Salt and pepper, to taste
- Pinch of cream of tartar (optional, for stabilizing egg whites)

Instructions:

1. Preheat oven: Preheat your oven to 375°F (190°C). Place a baking sheet in the oven to heat up.
2. Prepare soufflé dish: Generously butter a 1 1/2-quart (1.5-liter) soufflé dish. Coat the buttered dish with grated Parmesan cheese, tapping out any excess. This helps the soufflé to rise properly.
3. Make béchamel sauce: In a saucepan, melt 2 tablespoons of butter over medium heat. Stir in the flour and cook for 1-2 minutes, stirring constantly, to make a roux. Gradually whisk in the milk, stirring constantly, until the mixture thickens and comes to a boil. Remove from heat and stir in the grated Gruyère cheese until melted. Season with salt and pepper to taste. Let the mixture cool slightly.
4. Separate eggs: Separate the eggs, placing the yolks in a large mixing bowl and the whites in a clean, grease-free mixing bowl.
5. Mix egg yolks with béchamel: Whisk the egg yolks into the slightly cooled béchamel sauce until well combined.
6. Beat egg whites: Using an electric mixer, beat the egg whites until stiff peaks form. If desired, add a pinch of cream of tartar while beating to stabilize the egg whites.
7.
8. Combine mixtures: Gently fold one-third of the beaten egg whites into the egg yolk mixture to lighten it. Then, carefully fold in the remaining egg whites until no streaks remain. Be gentle to avoid deflating the egg whites.
9. Bake: Pour the soufflé mixture into the prepared soufflé dish, smoothing the top with a spatula. Run your thumb around the rim of the dish to create a slight

indentation, which helps the soufflé rise evenly. Place the soufflé dish on the preheated baking sheet in the oven.
10. Bake: Bake the soufflé for 25-30 minutes, or until puffed and golden brown on top. Avoid opening the oven door during baking, as this can cause the soufflé to deflate.
11. Serve immediately: Serve the soufflé immediately, straight from the oven, as it will begin to deflate as it cools. Enjoy the light and fluffy texture and the rich, cheesy flavor of this classic French dish!

Soufflés are a stunning addition to any meal, whether served as an elegant appetizer or a decadent dessert. Experiment with different flavors and ingredients to create your own signature soufflé recipes!

Tarte aux Fraises

Ingredients:

For the tart shell:

- 1 1/4 cups (160g) all-purpose flour
- 1/4 cup (50g) granulated sugar
- 1/2 cup (115g) unsalted butter, cold and cut into small cubes
- 1 large egg yolk
- 1-2 tablespoons cold water (as needed)

For the pastry cream:

- 1 cup (240ml) whole milk
- 1/2 cup (100g) granulated sugar
- 3 large egg yolks
- 2 tablespoons all-purpose flour
- 1 teaspoon vanilla extract

For assembling:

- 1 pound (450g) fresh strawberries, hulled and halved
- 1/4 cup (60ml) apricot jam, warmed (for glazing)

Instructions:

For the tart shell:

1. Prepare dough: In a food processor, combine the flour and sugar. Add the cold cubed butter and pulse until the mixture resembles coarse crumbs. Add the egg yolk and pulse again until the dough starts to come together. If the dough seems dry, add 1-2 tablespoons of cold water, one at a time, until it forms a ball.
2. Chill dough: Shape the dough into a disk, wrap it in plastic wrap, and refrigerate for at least 30 minutes.
3. Roll out dough: On a lightly floured surface, roll out the chilled dough into a circle large enough to fit your tart pan. Transfer the dough to a 9-inch (23cm) tart pan with a removable bottom. Press the dough into the bottom and sides of the pan, trimming any excess dough. Prick the bottom of the dough with a fork to prevent it from puffing up during baking. Chill the tart shell in the refrigerator for another 30 minutes.

4. **Preheat oven:** Preheat your oven to 375°F (190°C).
5. **Blind bake:** Line the chilled tart shell with parchment paper or aluminum foil and fill it with pie weights or dried beans. Bake in the preheated oven for about 15-20 minutes, or until the edges are lightly golden. Remove the parchment paper and weights and continue to bake for another 5-10 minutes, or until the bottom is fully cooked and golden brown. Remove from the oven and let it cool completely.

For the pastry cream:

1. **Heat milk:** In a saucepan, heat the whole milk over medium heat until it just starts to simmer.
2. **Mix egg yolks:** In a mixing bowl, whisk together the granulated sugar and egg yolks until pale and creamy. Add the flour and whisk until smooth.
3. **Temper eggs:** Gradually pour the hot milk into the egg mixture, whisking constantly, to temper the eggs.
4. **Cook mixture:** Return the mixture to the saucepan and cook over medium heat, stirring constantly, until it thickens and comes to a boil. Remove from heat and stir in the vanilla extract.
5. **Chill:** Transfer the pastry cream to a clean bowl and cover the surface with plastic wrap to prevent a skin from forming. Refrigerate until chilled and set.

Assembly:

1. **Fill tart shell:** Spread the chilled pastry cream evenly over the bottom of the cooled tart shell.
2. **Arrange strawberries:** Arrange the halved strawberries on top of the pastry cream in a decorative pattern.
3. **Glaze:** Using a pastry brush, gently brush the warmed apricot jam over the strawberries to glaze and add shine.
4. **Chill and serve:** Refrigerate the tart for at least 1 hour before serving to allow the flavors to meld. Serve chilled and enjoy!

Tarte aux Fraises is a delightful and elegant dessert that's perfect for showcasing the beauty and flavor of fresh strawberries. Enjoy it as a sweet treat for special occasions or as a refreshing dessert on a warm day!

Pâte de Fruits

Ingredients:

- 2 cups (400g) fruit puree (such as raspberry, strawberry, apricot, or any other fruit of your choice)
- 2 cups (400g) granulated sugar, plus extra for coating
- 1/4 cup (60ml) water
- 1/4 cup (60ml) freshly squeezed lemon juice
- 1 packet (about 1 ounce or 28g) powdered pectin
- Optional: Confectioners' sugar, for dusting

Instructions:

1. Prepare fruit puree: If using fresh fruit, wash and prepare it as needed, then puree it in a blender or food processor until smooth. Strain the puree through a fine-mesh sieve to remove any seeds or pulp. Measure out 2 cups of fruit puree.
2. Cook fruit puree: In a large, heavy-bottomed saucepan, combine the fruit puree, granulated sugar, water, and lemon juice. Stir to combine.
3. Add pectin: Sprinkle the powdered pectin evenly over the fruit mixture and stir until well combined.
4. Cook mixture: Place the saucepan over medium heat and bring the mixture to a boil, stirring frequently to dissolve the sugar and pectin.
5. Simmer: Once the mixture reaches a boil, reduce the heat to low and simmer, stirring occasionally, until the mixture thickens and reaches the gel stage. This can take anywhere from 20 to 30 minutes, depending on the fruit used.
6. Test for gel stage: To test if the mixture has reached the gel stage, you can perform a spoon test: Dip a metal spoon into the mixture and lift it out. If the mixture sheets off the spoon in a thick, syrupy consistency rather than dripping off in liquid form, it is ready.
7. Pour into molds: Once the mixture has reached the desired consistency, immediately pour it into silicone candy molds or a parchment-lined baking dish. Smooth the top with a spatula.
8. Cool and set: Let the Pâte de Fruits cool and set at room temperature for several hours, or preferably overnight, until firm and set.
9. Cut and coat: Once set, unmold the Pâte de Fruits from the molds or lift it out of the baking dish using the parchment paper. Cut the Pâte de Fruits into small squares or shapes using a sharp knife. Toss the pieces in granulated sugar to coat them evenly.

10. Store: Store the coated Pâte de Fruits in an airtight container at room temperature for up to two weeks. If desired, you can dust them with confectioners' sugar before serving.

Pâte de Fruits are a delightful and elegant confection that make a lovely gift or addition to a dessert platter. Enjoy the intense fruit flavor and chewy texture of these homemade treats!

Croquembouche

Ingredients:

For the choux pastry (profiteroles):

- 1 cup (240ml) water
- 1/2 cup (115g) unsalted butter
- 1 tablespoon granulated sugar
- 1/4 teaspoon salt
- 1 cup (125g) all-purpose flour
- 4 large eggs

For the pastry cream filling:

- 2 cups (480ml) whole milk
- 1/2 cup (100g) granulated sugar
- 4 large egg yolks
- 1/4 cup (30g) cornstarch
- 1 teaspoon vanilla extract

For assembling:

- Caramelized sugar (for assembling the tower)
- Optional: Candied nuts, chocolate drizzle, or decorative elements

Instructions:

For the choux pastry (profiteroles):

1. Preheat oven: Preheat your oven to 425°F (220°C). Line a baking sheet with parchment paper or a silicone baking mat.
2. Prepare dough: In a saucepan, combine water, butter, sugar, and salt. Bring to a boil over medium heat. Remove from heat and add flour all at once. Stir vigorously with a wooden spoon until the mixture forms a ball and pulls away from the sides of the pan.
3. Add eggs: Transfer the dough to a mixing bowl. Let it cool for a few minutes. Beat in the eggs, one at a time, mixing well after each addition, until the dough is smooth and glossy.

4. Pipe dough: Transfer the dough to a pastry bag fitted with a large round tip. Pipe small mounds (about 1 inch in diameter) onto the prepared baking sheet, spacing them a couple of inches apart.
5. Bake: Bake in the preheated oven for 15 minutes. Reduce the oven temperature to 375°F (190°C) and continue to bake for another 20-25 minutes, or until the profiteroles are golden brown and puffed. Remove from the oven and let them cool completely.

For the pastry cream filling:

1. Heat milk: In a saucepan, heat the whole milk over medium heat until it just starts to simmer.
2. Mix egg yolks: In a mixing bowl, whisk together the granulated sugar and egg yolks until pale and creamy. Add the cornstarch and whisk until smooth.
3. Temper eggs: Gradually pour the hot milk into the egg mixture, whisking constantly, to temper the eggs.
4. Cook mixture: Return the mixture to the saucepan and cook over medium heat, stirring constantly, until it thickens and comes to a boil. Remove from heat and stir in the vanilla extract.
5. Chill: Transfer the pastry cream to a clean bowl and cover the surface with plastic wrap to prevent a skin from forming. Refrigerate until chilled and set.

For assembling:

1. Fill profiteroles: Fill the cooled profiteroles with the chilled pastry cream using a piping bag fitted with a small round tip. Alternatively, you can slice each profiterole in half and spoon the cream inside.
2. Assemble tower: Dip the bottom of each filled profiterole into caramelized sugar and arrange them in a cone shape on a serving platter or cake stand, stacking them one on top of the other to form a tower.
3. Decorate: Drizzle additional caramelized sugar over the top of the Croquembouche to create decorative threads or strands. You can also garnish with candied nuts, chocolate drizzle, or other decorative elements as desired.
4. Serve: Serve the Croquembouche immediately as an impressive and elegant dessert centerpiece. To serve, simply pull off individual profiteroles from the tower.

Croquembouche is a show-stopping dessert that's sure to impress guests at any special occasion. Enjoy the crisp, caramelized exterior of the profiteroles paired with the creamy pastry cream filling for a delightful and indulgent treat!

Tarte au Citron

Ingredients:

For the pastry crust:

- 1 1/4 cups (160g) all-purpose flour
- 1/4 cup (30g) powdered sugar
- 1/2 cup (115g) unsalted butter, cold and cut into small cubes
- 1 large egg yolk
- 1-2 tablespoons ice water (as needed)

For the lemon filling:

- 4-5 large lemons (about 1 cup/240ml lemon juice)
- Zest of 2 lemons
- 1 cup (200g) granulated sugar
- 4 large eggs
- 1/2 cup (115g) unsalted butter, melted and cooled
- Optional: Confectioners' sugar, for dusting

Instructions:

For the pastry crust:

1. Prepare dough: In a food processor, combine the flour and powdered sugar. Add the cold cubed butter and pulse until the mixture resembles coarse crumbs. Add the egg yolk and pulse again until the dough starts to come together. If the dough seems dry, add 1-2 tablespoons of ice water, one at a time, until it forms a ball.
2. Chill dough: Shape the dough into a disk, wrap it in plastic wrap, and refrigerate for at least 30 minutes.
3. Roll out dough: On a lightly floured surface, roll out the chilled dough into a circle large enough to fit your tart pan. Transfer the dough to a 9-inch (23cm) tart pan with a removable bottom. Press the dough into the bottom and sides of the pan, trimming any excess dough. Prick the bottom of the dough with a fork to prevent it from puffing up during baking. Chill the tart shell in the refrigerator for another 30 minutes.
4. Preheat oven: Preheat your oven to 375°F (190°C).
5. Blind bake: Line the chilled tart shell with parchment paper or aluminum foil and fill it with pie weights or dried beans. Bake in the preheated oven for about 15-20 minutes, or until the edges are lightly golden. Remove the parchment paper and

weights and continue to bake for another 5-10 minutes, or until the bottom is fully cooked and golden brown. Remove from the oven and let it cool completely.

For the lemon filling:

1. Prepare lemons: Zest and juice the lemons, straining the juice to remove any seeds and pulp. You'll need about 1 cup (240ml) of lemon juice.
2. Mix filling: In a mixing bowl, whisk together the granulated sugar, lemon zest, and eggs until well combined. Gradually whisk in the lemon juice until smooth. Finally, whisk in the melted butter until the mixture is smooth and well combined.
3. Cook mixture: Pour the lemon filling into a saucepan and cook over medium heat, stirring constantly, until the mixture thickens and coats the back of a spoon. This usually takes about 5-7 minutes.
4. Cool: Remove the lemon filling from heat and let it cool slightly.

Assembly:

1. Fill tart shell: Pour the slightly cooled lemon filling into the cooled tart shell, spreading it out evenly.
2. Chill: Refrigerate the tart for at least 2 hours, or until the filling is set.
3. Serve: Serve the Tarte au Citron chilled, dusted with confectioners' sugar if desired.

Tarte au Citron is a delightful and elegant dessert that's perfect for any occasion. Enjoy the bright and refreshing flavor of lemon paired with the buttery richness of the pastry crust for a truly indulgent treat!

Gâteau Basque

Ingredients:

For the pastry dough:

- 2 cups (250g) all-purpose flour
- 1 teaspoon baking powder
- 1/2 teaspoon salt
- 1 cup (225g) unsalted butter, softened
- 1 cup (200g) granulated sugar
- 2 large eggs
- 1 teaspoon vanilla extract (or almond extract, if preferred)
- Zest of 1 lemon (optional)

For the filling:

- 1 1/4 cups (150g) ground almonds (or almond flour)
- 3/4 cup (150g) granulated sugar
- 2 large egg yolks
- 1 teaspoon vanilla extract (or almond extract)
- Zest of 1 lemon (optional)
- 1/4 cup (60ml) heavy cream

For assembling:

- 1 large egg, beaten (for egg wash)
- Powdered sugar, for dusting

Instructions:

For the pastry dough:

1. Mix dry ingredients: In a mixing bowl, whisk together the flour, baking powder, and salt.
2. Cream butter and sugar: In a separate mixing bowl, cream together the softened butter and granulated sugar until light and fluffy.
3. Add eggs and flavorings: Add the eggs one at a time, beating well after each addition. Mix in the vanilla extract (or almond extract) and lemon zest, if using.
4. Combine wet and dry ingredients: Gradually add the dry ingredients to the wet ingredients, mixing until a smooth dough forms. Divide the dough into two equal

portions, shape each portion into a disk, wrap them in plastic wrap, and refrigerate for at least 1 hour, or until firm.

For the filling:

1. Mix ingredients: In a mixing bowl, combine the ground almonds, granulated sugar, egg yolks, vanilla extract (or almond extract), lemon zest (if using), and heavy cream. Mix until well combined to form a thick, paste-like filling.

For assembling:

1. Preheat oven: Preheat your oven to 350°F (175°C). Grease and line the bottom of a 9-inch (23cm) round cake pan with parchment paper.
2. Roll out dough: On a lightly floured surface, roll out one portion of the chilled pastry dough into a circle large enough to line the bottom and sides of the prepared cake pan. Press the dough into the bottom and sides of the pan, making sure to evenly distribute the dough.
3. Fill with almond mixture: Spread the almond filling evenly over the bottom of the pastry dough in the cake pan.
4. Top with second layer of dough: Roll out the second portion of chilled pastry dough into a circle large enough to cover the filling and fit the top of the cake pan. Carefully place it over the almond filling, pressing the edges to seal with the bottom crust.
5. Brush with egg wash: Brush the top of the pastry dough with beaten egg to create a shiny, golden finish.
6. Bake: Bake in the preheated oven for 30-35 minutes, or until the pastry is golden brown and cooked through.
7. Cool and serve: Remove the Gâteau Basque from the oven and let it cool in the pan for 10-15 minutes. Then, transfer it to a wire rack to cool completely. Once cooled, dust with powdered sugar before serving.

Gâteau Basque is best served at room temperature. Enjoy slices of this delicious dessert with a cup of coffee or tea for a delightful treat!

Chouquettes

Ingredients:

- 1/2 cup (120ml) water
- 1/2 cup (120ml) whole milk
- 1/2 cup (115g) unsalted butter, cut into small pieces
- 1 tablespoon granulated sugar
- 1/4 teaspoon salt
- 1 cup (125g) all-purpose flour
- 4 large eggs, at room temperature
- Pearl sugar, for topping

Instructions:

1. Preheat oven: Preheat your oven to 425°F (220°C). Line a baking sheet with parchment paper or a silicone baking mat.
2. Prepare dough: In a saucepan, combine water, milk, butter, sugar, and salt. Bring to a boil over medium heat, stirring occasionally.
3. Add flour: Once the mixture comes to a boil, remove from heat and add the flour all at once. Stir vigorously with a wooden spoon until the mixture forms a smooth, thick dough.
4. Cool: Transfer the dough to a mixing bowl and let it cool for a few minutes.
5. Add eggs: Add the eggs to the dough, one at a time, beating well after each addition, until the dough is smooth and glossy. It should be thick enough to hold its shape when piped.
6. Pipe dough: Transfer the dough to a piping bag fitted with a large round tip (or simply snip off the end of a plastic bag). Pipe small mounds of dough onto the prepared baking sheet, leaving space between each mound for spreading.
7. Top with pearl sugar: Sprinkle pearl sugar generously over the piped dough mounds.
8. Bake: Bake in the preheated oven for 15-20 minutes, or until the chouquettes are puffed up and golden brown.
9. Cool: Remove from the oven and let the chouquettes cool on the baking sheet for a few minutes before transferring them to a wire rack to cool completely.
10. Serve: Serve the chouquettes as a delightful snack or dessert. They are best enjoyed fresh on the day they are made.

Chouquettes are versatile pastries that can be enjoyed on their own or filled with whipped cream, pastry cream, or other fillings for a more decadent treat. Enjoy these light and airy pastries with a cup of coffee or tea for a delightful French experience!

Pain d'Épices

Ingredients:

- 2 cups (250g) all-purpose flour
- 1 teaspoon baking powder
- 1 teaspoon ground cinnamon
- 1/2 teaspoon ground ginger
- 1/4 teaspoon ground cloves
- 1/4 teaspoon ground nutmeg
- Pinch of salt
- 1/2 cup (120ml) whole milk
- 1/2 cup (120ml) honey
- 1/4 cup (50g) granulated sugar
- 1 large egg
- Zest of 1 orange (optional)
- Zest of 1 lemon (optional)

Instructions:

1. Preheat oven: Preheat your oven to 350°F (175°C). Grease and flour a 9x5-inch (23x13cm) loaf pan, or line it with parchment paper.
2. Mix dry ingredients: In a mixing bowl, whisk together the flour, baking powder, ground cinnamon, ground ginger, ground cloves, ground nutmeg, and salt until well combined.
3. Warm honey: In a small saucepan, gently warm the honey over low heat until it becomes more fluid. Be careful not to let it boil.
4. Combine wet ingredients: In a separate mixing bowl, whisk together the warm honey, whole milk, granulated sugar, egg, and optional orange and lemon zest until well combined.
5. Combine wet and dry ingredients: Gradually add the dry ingredients to the wet ingredients, mixing until just combined. Be careful not to overmix.
6. Bake: Pour the batter into the prepared loaf pan and smooth the top with a spatula. Bake in the preheated oven for 45-50 minutes, or until a toothpick inserted into the center comes out clean.
7. Cool: Remove the Pain d'Épices from the oven and let it cool in the pan for 10 minutes. Then, transfer it to a wire rack to cool completely.
8. Serve: Once cooled, slice the Pain d'Épices and serve it as a delightful treat with a cup of tea or coffee.

Pain d'Épices can be enjoyed plain or spread with butter or jam for added flavor. It also pairs well with cheese or foie gras for a savory-sweet combination. Enjoy the rich, spiced flavor of this classic French treat!

Far Breton

Ingredients:

- 1 cup (125g) all-purpose flour
- 1/2 cup (100g) granulated sugar
- Pinch of salt
- 4 large eggs
- 2 cups (480ml) whole milk
- 1 teaspoon vanilla extract
- 1/4 cup (60ml) rum (optional)
- 1 cup (150g) pitted prunes (optional)
- Butter or oil, for greasing

Instructions:

1. Prepare prunes (optional): If using prunes, place them in a small bowl and cover them with rum. Let them soak for at least 30 minutes to plump up.
2. Preheat oven: Preheat your oven to 350°F (175°C). Grease a 9-inch (23cm) round baking dish with butter or oil.
3. Mix dry ingredients: In a mixing bowl, whisk together the flour, sugar, and salt until well combined.
4. Add wet ingredients: In a separate mixing bowl, whisk together the eggs, whole milk, and vanilla extract until well combined.
5. Combine wet and dry ingredients: Gradually add the wet ingredients to the dry ingredients, whisking until smooth and no lumps remain.
6. Add prunes (optional): If using soaked prunes, drain them and arrange them evenly in the bottom of the prepared baking dish.
7. Pour batter: Pour the batter over the prunes (if using) or directly into the prepared baking dish.
8. Bake: Bake in the preheated oven for 45-50 minutes, or until the Far Breton is set and golden brown on top. It should have a slight jiggle in the center but not be liquidy.
9. Cool: Remove the Far Breton from the oven and let it cool in the baking dish for at least 10-15 minutes before serving.
10. Serve: Slice the Far Breton into wedges and serve warm or at room temperature. It can be enjoyed on its own or dusted with powdered sugar for added sweetness.

Far Breton is a comforting and satisfying dessert that's perfect for any occasion. Its creamy texture and subtle sweetness make it a favorite among both children and adults. Enjoy it as a delightful treat with a cup of tea or coffee!

Crêpes Suzette

Ingredients:

For the crêpes:

- 1 cup (125g) all-purpose flour
- 2 large eggs
- 1 cup (240ml) whole milk
- 1/4 cup (60ml) water
- 2 tablespoons unsalted butter, melted
- 1 tablespoon granulated sugar
- Pinch of salt
- Butter or oil, for cooking

For the Suzette sauce:

- 1/2 cup (100g) granulated sugar
- Zest of 1 orange
- 1/2 cup (120ml) freshly squeezed orange juice
- 1/4 cup (60ml) Grand Marnier or orange liqueur
- 4 tablespoons unsalted butter, cubed
- Orange segments, for garnish (optional)

Instructions:

For the crêpes:

1. Make batter: In a mixing bowl, whisk together the flour, eggs, whole milk, water, melted butter, sugar, and salt until smooth and well combined. Let the batter rest for at least 30 minutes at room temperature.
2. Cook crêpes: Heat a non-stick skillet or crêpe pan over medium heat. Brush the pan with a little butter or oil. Pour a small ladleful of batter into the pan, swirling it around to coat the bottom evenly. Cook for about 1-2 minutes, or until the edges start to lift and the bottom is golden brown. Flip the crêpe and cook for another 1-2 minutes on the other side. Repeat with the remaining batter, stacking the cooked crêpes on a plate as you go.

For the Suzette sauce:

1. Prepare sauce: In a large skillet or flambé pan, combine the granulated sugar and orange zest. Cook over medium heat, stirring constantly, until the sugar melts and caramelizes to a golden brown color.
2. Deglaze: Carefully add the freshly squeezed orange juice to the caramelized sugar, stirring constantly to dissolve any caramelized bits.
3. Add liqueur and butter: Stir in the Grand Marnier or orange liqueur until well combined. Gradually add the cubed butter, stirring continuously, until the sauce is smooth and glossy.
4. Flambé: Carefully place one crêpe at a time into the sauce, folding it into quarters or rolling it into a cylinder. Allow each crêpe to soak up some of the sauce before transferring it to a serving plate. Repeat with the remaining crêpes. Once all the crêpes are in the sauce, carefully ignite the sauce with a long match or lighter. Allow the flames to die down before serving.
5. Serve: Garnish the Crêpes Suzette with orange segments, if desired. Serve immediately while still warm.

Crêpes Suzette is a decadent and elegant dessert that's sure to impress guests with its dramatic presentation and delicious flavor. Enjoy it as a special treat for brunch, dessert, or any festive occasion!

Chaussons aux Pommes

Ingredients:

For the pastry dough:

- 2 cups (250g) all-purpose flour
- 1/2 teaspoon salt
- 1 tablespoon granulated sugar
- 1 cup (225g) unsalted butter, cold and cut into small cubes
- 1/2 cup (120ml) cold water

For the apple filling:

- 3 large apples (such as Granny Smith or Gala), peeled, cored, and diced
- 1/4 cup (50g) granulated sugar
- 1 teaspoon ground cinnamon
- 1/4 teaspoon ground nutmeg
- 1 tablespoon lemon juice
- 2 tablespoons unsalted butter

For assembling:

- 1 large egg, beaten (for egg wash)
- Granulated sugar, for sprinkling

Instructions:

For the pastry dough:

1. Prepare dough: In a mixing bowl, whisk together the flour, salt, and sugar. Add the cold cubed butter and use a pastry cutter or your fingertips to work the butter into the flour mixture until it resembles coarse crumbs.
2. Add water: Gradually add the cold water, a little at a time, mixing with a fork until the dough starts to come together. Be careful not to overwork the dough.
3. Form dough: Turn the dough out onto a lightly floured surface and knead it gently a few times until it forms a cohesive ball. Flatten the dough into a disk, wrap it in plastic wrap, and refrigerate for at least 30 minutes to chill.

For the apple filling:

1. Cook apples: In a saucepan, combine the diced apples, granulated sugar, ground cinnamon, ground nutmeg, and lemon juice. Cook over medium heat, stirring occasionally, until the apples are soft and tender, about 8-10 minutes.
2. Mash apples: Once the apples are cooked, use a potato masher or fork to mash them slightly to create a chunky applesauce consistency. Remove from heat and stir in the unsalted butter until melted and well combined. Let the filling cool slightly.

For assembling:

1. Preheat oven: Preheat your oven to 375°F (190°C). Line a baking sheet with parchment paper or a silicone baking mat.
2. Roll out dough: On a lightly floured surface, roll out the chilled dough into a large circle, about 1/8 inch (3mm) thick. Use a sharp knife or pastry cutter to cut the dough into 6-8 equal-sized circles.
3. Fill and fold: Spoon a generous spoonful of the apple filling onto one half of each dough circle, leaving a border around the edges. Fold the other half of the dough over the filling to create a half-moon shape. Press the edges firmly to seal, then crimp the edges with a fork to secure.
4. Brush with egg wash: Place the filled turnovers onto the prepared baking sheet. Brush the tops of the turnovers with beaten egg, then sprinkle them with granulated sugar for added sweetness and crunch.
5. Bake: Bake in the preheated oven for 20-25 minutes, or until the turnovers are golden brown and crisp.
6. Cool and serve: Remove the Chaussons aux Pommes from the oven and let them cool on the baking sheet for a few minutes before transferring them to a wire rack to cool completely. Serve warm or at room temperature.

Chaussons aux Pommes are best enjoyed fresh on the day they are made, but they can be stored in an airtight container at room temperature for up to 2 days. They are delicious served with a dollop of whipped cream or a scoop of vanilla ice cream for an extra special treat!

Tarte Tropézienne

Ingredients:

For the brioche dough:

- 2 cups (250g) all-purpose flour
- 1/4 cup (50g) granulated sugar
- 1 teaspoon active dry yeast
- 1/2 teaspoon salt
- 3 large eggs, at room temperature
- 1/2 cup (115g) unsalted butter, softened
- 1/4 cup (60ml) warm milk
- 1 teaspoon vanilla extract

For the pastry cream:

- 1 cup (240ml) whole milk
- 4 large egg yolks
- 1/4 cup (50g) granulated sugar
- 2 tablespoons cornstarch
- 1 teaspoon vanilla extract
- 1 cup (240ml) heavy cream

For the sugar glaze:

- 1/2 cup (100g) granulated sugar
- 1/4 cup (60ml) water

Additional:

- Powdered sugar, for dusting

Instructions:

For the brioche dough:

1. Activate yeast: In a small bowl, dissolve the yeast in the warm milk and let it sit for 5-10 minutes until foamy.
2. Mix dry ingredients: In a large mixing bowl, combine the flour, sugar, and salt.

3. Combine wet ingredients: Make a well in the center of the dry ingredients and add the activated yeast mixture, eggs, and vanilla extract. Mix until a rough dough forms.
4. Knead: Turn the dough out onto a floured surface and knead for about 10 minutes, or until the dough is smooth and elastic.
5. Incorporate butter: Gradually add the softened butter to the dough, a little at a time, kneading well after each addition until all the butter is incorporated and the dough is smooth and shiny.
6. First rise: Place the dough in a greased bowl, cover with plastic wrap, and let it rise in a warm place for about 1-2 hours, or until doubled in size.
7. Shape: Punch down the risen dough and divide it into two equal portions. Shape each portion into a ball and place them on a parchment-lined baking sheet, spaced apart. Cover with plastic wrap and let them rise for another 1-2 hours.
8. Bake: Preheat your oven to 350°F (175°C). Bake the brioche balls for 20-25 minutes, or until golden brown and cooked through. Let them cool completely on a wire rack.

For the pastry cream:

1. Heat milk: In a saucepan, heat the whole milk over medium heat until it just starts to simmer.
2. Mix egg yolks: In a mixing bowl, whisk together the egg yolks and granulated sugar until pale and creamy. Add the cornstarch and whisk until smooth.
3. Temper eggs: Gradually pour the hot milk into the egg mixture, whisking constantly, to temper the eggs.
4. Cook mixture: Return the mixture to the saucepan and cook over medium heat, stirring constantly, until it thickens and comes to a boil. Remove from heat and stir in the vanilla extract.
5. Chill: Transfer the pastry cream to a clean bowl and cover the surface with plastic wrap to prevent a skin from forming. Refrigerate until chilled.
6. Whip cream: In a separate mixing bowl, whip the heavy cream until stiff peaks form. Gently fold the whipped cream into the chilled pastry cream until well combined.

For the sugar glaze:

1. Make glaze: In a small saucepan, combine the granulated sugar and water. Bring to a boil over medium heat, stirring occasionally, until the sugar is completely dissolved. Remove from heat and let the glaze cool slightly.

Assembly:

1. Slice brioche: Using a serrated knife, slice each brioche ball horizontally into two equal layers.
2. Fill: Spread a generous layer of the prepared pastry cream onto the bottom half of each brioche.
3. Assemble: Place the top half of each brioche over the pastry cream to sandwich them together.
4. Glaze: Brush the sugar glaze over the top of each assembled Tarte Tropézienne.
5. Chill: Refrigerate the assembled tarts for at least 1 hour to allow the flavors to meld and the glaze to set.
6. Serve: Dust the Tarte Tropézienne with powdered sugar before serving. Slice and enjoy!

Tarte Tropézienne is a delightful and indulgent dessert that's perfect for any occasion. Its creamy filling and sweet glaze pair perfectly with the buttery brioche, creating a truly irresistible treat.

Île Flottante

Ingredients:

For the custard:

- 2 cups (480ml) whole milk
- 1 vanilla bean or 1 teaspoon vanilla extract
- 4 large egg yolks
- 1/3 cup (65g) granulated sugar

For the meringue:

- 4 large egg whites, at room temperature
- Pinch of salt
- 1/4 cup (50g) granulated sugar

For the caramel sauce (optional):

- 1 cup (200g) granulated sugar
- 1/4 cup (60ml) water
- 1/2 cup (120ml) heavy cream
- 1 tablespoon unsalted butter

Instructions:

For the custard:

1. Prepare custard base: In a saucepan, heat the whole milk over medium heat until it just starts to simmer. Remove from heat.
2. Infuse vanilla: If using a vanilla bean, split it lengthwise and scrape the seeds into the warm milk. Add the vanilla bean pod as well. Let it steep for 15-20 minutes to infuse the flavor. If using vanilla extract, simply add it to the warm milk.
3. Make custard: In a mixing bowl, whisk together the egg yolks and granulated sugar until pale and creamy. Gradually pour the warm milk into the egg mixture, whisking constantly to temper the eggs.
4. Cook custard: Return the mixture to the saucepan and cook over low heat, stirring constantly with a wooden spoon, until the custard thickens enough to coat the back of the spoon. Do not let it boil.

5. Strain and chill: Strain the custard through a fine-mesh sieve into a clean bowl to remove any lumps and the vanilla bean pod (if using). Cover the surface of the custard with plastic wrap to prevent a skin from forming. Refrigerate until chilled.

For the meringue:

1. Whip egg whites: In a clean, dry mixing bowl, beat the egg whites with a pinch of salt using a hand mixer or stand mixer until soft peaks form.
2. Gradually add sugar: Gradually add the granulated sugar, a little at a time, while continuing to beat the egg whites, until stiff peaks form and the meringue is glossy.
3. Poach meringue: Bring a large pot of water to a gentle simmer. Using two large spoons, shape the meringue into oval-shaped quenelles and gently lower them into the simmering water. Poach the meringues for about 2-3 minutes on each side, until they are firm and set.
4. Drain and cool: Using a slotted spoon, transfer the poached meringues to a plate lined with paper towels to drain excess water. Let them cool completely.

For the caramel sauce (optional):

1. Make caramel: In a saucepan, combine the granulated sugar and water over medium heat, stirring until the sugar dissolves. Stop stirring and let the mixture boil until it turns a deep amber color, swirling the pan occasionally to ensure even caramelization.
2. Add cream and butter: Carefully add the heavy cream to the caramel (it will bubble vigorously) and whisk until smooth. Remove from heat and stir in the butter until melted and combined.

Assembly:

1. Serve: To serve, divide the chilled custard among serving bowls or plates. Place the poached meringues on top of the custard.
2. Drizzle with caramel sauce: If using caramel sauce, drizzle it over the poached meringues and custard.
3. Garnish: Optionally, garnish with toasted almonds, grated chocolate, or fresh berries.
4. Serve: Serve Île Flottante immediately, or refrigerate until ready to serve.

Île Flottante is a delightful and elegant dessert that's perfect for special occasions or when you're craving something light and sweet. Enjoy the contrast of the airy meringue against the creamy custard, with the added richness of caramel sauce if desired!

Quatre-Quarts

Ingredients:

- 4 large eggs, at room temperature
- Equal weight of:
    - Unsalted butter, softened
    - Granulated sugar
    - All-purpose flour
- 1 teaspoon baking powder
- Pinch of salt
- 1 teaspoon vanilla extract (optional)

Instructions:

1. Preheat oven and prepare pan: Preheat your oven to 350°F (175°C). Grease and flour a 9x5-inch (23x13cm) loaf pan, or line it with parchment paper.
2. Cream butter and sugar: In a mixing bowl, cream together the softened butter and granulated sugar until light and fluffy.
3. Add eggs: Add the eggs one at a time, beating well after each addition. If using vanilla extract, add it with the last egg.
4. Combine dry ingredients: In a separate bowl, sift together the all-purpose flour, baking powder, and salt.
5. Incorporate dry ingredients: Gradually add the dry ingredients to the butter mixture, mixing until just combined. Be careful not to overmix.
6. Pour batter into pan: Pour the batter into the prepared loaf pan and smooth the top with a spatula.
7. Bake: Bake in the preheated oven for 45-55 minutes, or until a toothpick inserted into the center comes out clean and the top is golden brown.
8. Cool: Remove the Quatre-Quarts from the oven and let it cool in the pan for 10-15 minutes. Then, transfer it to a wire rack to cool completely.
9. Serve: Once cooled, slice the Quatre-Quarts and serve it as a delightful treat with a cup of tea or coffee.

Quatre-Quarts is a versatile cake that can be enjoyed plain or with a dusting of powdered sugar. You can also add flavor variations such as lemon zest, almond extract, or chocolate chips to customize it to your liking. It's perfect for any occasion, from breakfast to dessert!

Kouign-Amann

Ingredients:

For the dough:

- 2 cups (250g) all-purpose flour, plus extra for dusting
- 1 teaspoon active dry yeast
- 1/2 teaspoon salt
- 3/4 cup (180ml) lukewarm water
- 1/4 cup (50g) unsalted butter, melted

For the butter block:

- 1 cup (225g) unsalted butter, cold

For the sugar filling:

- 1 cup (200g) granulated sugar, plus extra for sprinkling

Instructions:

For the dough:

1. Activate yeast: In a small bowl, dissolve the yeast in the lukewarm water and let it sit for 5-10 minutes until foamy.
2. Mix dough: In a large mixing bowl, combine the flour and salt. Add the activated yeast mixture and melted butter to the flour mixture. Mix until a rough dough forms.
3. Knead: Turn the dough out onto a lightly floured surface and knead for about 5-7 minutes, or until the dough is smooth and elastic. Shape the dough into a ball.
4. First rise: Place the dough in a lightly greased bowl, cover with plastic wrap, and let it rise in a warm place for about 1-2 hours, or until doubled in size.

For the butter block:

1. Prepare butter: Place the cold unsalted butter between two sheets of parchment paper or plastic wrap. Use a rolling pin to flatten and shape the butter into a rectangle, about 1/2 inch (1.25cm) thick. Chill the butter block in the refrigerator until firm.

Assembly:

1. Roll out dough: On a lightly floured surface, roll out the risen dough into a large rectangle, about 1/4 inch (0.6cm) thick.
2. Add butter block: Place the chilled butter block in the center of the rolled-out dough. Fold the edges of the dough over the butter block to encase it completely, sealing the edges tightly.
3. Roll and fold: Roll out the dough into a long rectangle, about 1/4 inch (0.6cm) thick. Fold the dough into thirds like a letter (known as a "turn"). Rotate the dough 90 degrees and repeat the rolling and folding process two more times, for a total of three turns.
4. Chill: Wrap the folded dough in plastic wrap and refrigerate for at least 30 minutes to relax the gluten and firm up the butter.
5. Prepare sugar filling: In a small bowl, mix together the granulated sugar with a pinch of salt.
6. Shape Kouign-Amann: On a lightly floured surface, roll out the chilled dough into a large rectangle, about 1/4 inch (0.6cm) thick. Sprinkle the sugar filling evenly over the dough, pressing it gently into the surface.
7. Fold and shape: Starting from one long edge, tightly roll up the dough into a log. Use a sharp knife to cut the log into even-sized slices, about 1 inch (2.5cm) thick.
8. Arrange in pan: Grease a muffin tin or individual ramekins with butter. Place each slice of dough into the prepared tin or ramekin, with the spiral side facing up. Sprinkle the tops with additional granulated sugar.
9. Second rise: Cover the shaped Kouign-Amann with a clean kitchen towel and let them rise in a warm place for about 30-45 minutes, or until puffed up and doubled in size.
10. Preheat oven: Preheat your oven to 375°F (190°C).
11. Bake: Bake the risen Kouign-Amann in the preheated oven for 25-30 minutes, or until golden brown and caramelized on the outside.
12. Cool and serve: Remove the Kouign-Amann from the oven and let them cool in the pan for a few minutes before transferring them to a wire rack to cool completely. Serve warm or at room temperature.

Kouign-Amann is best enjoyed fresh on the day it's made, while the caramelized exterior is still crisp and the layers of dough are soft and flaky. It's a delightful pastry that's perfect for breakfast, brunch, or dessert!

Gâteau Opéra

Ingredients:

For the Joconde (Almond Sponge Cake):

- 3 large eggs
- 1/2 cup (100g) granulated sugar
- 1/2 cup (60g) almond flour
- 1/4 cup (30g) all-purpose flour
- 2 tablespoons unsalted butter, melted and cooled
- 2 tablespoons warm water
- 1/2 teaspoon vanilla extract
- Pinch of salt

For the coffee syrup:

- 1/2 cup (120ml) strong brewed coffee
- 1/4 cup (50g) granulated sugar

For the coffee buttercream:

- 1/2 cup (115g) unsalted butter, softened
- 1 1/2 cups (180g) powdered sugar
- 1 tablespoon strong brewed coffee, cooled

For the chocolate ganache:

- 4 ounces (115g) semi-sweet chocolate, chopped
- 1/2 cup (120ml) heavy cream

For assembly:

- 2 tablespoons cocoa powder, for dusting

Instructions:

For the Joconde (Almond Sponge Cake):

1. Preheat oven: Preheat your oven to 350°F (175°C). Grease and line a 9x13-inch (23x33cm) baking pan with parchment paper.

2. Prepare batter: In a mixing bowl, beat the eggs and granulated sugar until pale and thick, about 5 minutes. Add the almond flour, all-purpose flour, melted butter, warm water, vanilla extract, and salt. Gently fold until well combined.
3. Bake: Pour the batter into the prepared baking pan and spread it evenly. Bake in the preheated oven for 10-12 minutes, or until the cake is golden and springs back when lightly pressed. Remove from the oven and let it cool in the pan for a few minutes before transferring it to a wire rack to cool completely.

For the coffee syrup:

1. Prepare syrup: In a small saucepan, combine the strong brewed coffee and granulated sugar. Heat over medium heat, stirring occasionally, until the sugar is dissolved. Remove from heat and let the syrup cool completely.

For the coffee buttercream:

1. Make buttercream: In a mixing bowl, beat the softened butter until creamy. Gradually add the powdered sugar, beating until light and fluffy. Add the cooled brewed coffee and beat until smooth and well combined.

For the chocolate ganache:

1. Prepare ganache: Place the chopped chocolate in a heatproof bowl. In a small saucepan, heat the heavy cream over medium heat until it just starts to simmer. Pour the hot cream over the chopped chocolate and let it sit for 1-2 minutes. Stir until the chocolate is melted and the ganache is smooth and glossy. Let it cool slightly.

Assembly:

1. Slice cake: Once the Joconde cake has cooled completely, use a sharp knife to carefully trim the edges and cut it into three equal-sized rectangles.
2. Layer cake: Place one layer of the Joconde cake on a serving platter or cake stand. Brush the surface generously with the coffee syrup.
3. Spread buttercream: Spread a layer of coffee buttercream evenly over the soaked cake layer.
4. Repeat layers: Place another layer of Joconde cake on top of the buttercream and brush it with coffee syrup. Spread another layer of buttercream on top.
5. Top with final layer: Place the last layer of Joconde cake on top and brush it with the remaining coffee syrup.

6. Cover with ganache: Pour the chocolate ganache over the top layer of the cake, allowing it to drip down the sides and spread it evenly with a spatula.
7. Chill: Refrigerate the assembled Gâteau Opéra for at least 1-2 hours, or until the ganache is set.
8. Finish: Before serving, dust the top of the cake with cocoa powder for decoration.

Gâteau Opéra is a stunning dessert that's sure to impress with its intricate layers and rich flavors. Serve it chilled and enjoy the harmonious combination of coffee, almond, and chocolate!

Bûche de Noël

Ingredients:

For the sponge cake:

- 4 large eggs, at room temperature
- 1/2 cup (100g) granulated sugar
- 1/2 cup (60g) cake flour
- 1/4 cup (30g) unsweetened cocoa powder
- 1/4 teaspoon salt
- 1 teaspoon vanilla extract

For the filling (choose one):

- Chocolate ganache
- Buttercream (flavored with chocolate, coffee, or vanilla)

For the chocolate ganache:

- 8 ounces (225g) semi-sweet chocolate, chopped
- 1 cup (240ml) heavy cream

For the buttercream:

- 1 cup (225g) unsalted butter, softened
- 2 cups (240g) powdered sugar
- 1 teaspoon vanilla extract (or other flavoring such as coffee or chocolate)

For decoration:

- Additional powdered sugar, for dusting
- Chocolate shavings
- Meringue mushrooms (optional)
- Marzipan decorations (optional)

Instructions:

For the sponge cake:

1. Preheat oven and prepare pan: Preheat your oven to 350°F (175°C). Grease a 10x15-inch (25x38cm) jelly roll pan and line it with parchment paper.

2. **Beat eggs:** In a mixing bowl, beat the eggs and granulated sugar together using a hand mixer or stand mixer until pale and fluffy, about 5 minutes.
3. **Sift dry ingredients:** In a separate bowl, sift together the cake flour, cocoa powder, and salt.
4. **Fold dry ingredients:** Gradually fold the sifted dry ingredients into the egg mixture using a spatula until just combined. Be gentle to avoid deflating the batter.
5. **Add vanilla extract:** Stir in the vanilla extract until evenly distributed.
6. **Bake:** Pour the batter into the prepared jelly roll pan and spread it evenly with a spatula. Bake in the preheated oven for 12-15 minutes, or until the cake springs back when lightly pressed.
7. **Roll cake:** While the cake is still warm, gently roll it up along the short edge with the parchment paper. Let it cool completely while rolled up.

For the filling:

1. **Prepare filling:** Choose either chocolate ganache or buttercream for the filling. If making chocolate ganache, heat the heavy cream in a saucepan until it just starts to simmer. Pour it over the chopped chocolate and let it sit for a few minutes. Stir until smooth and let it cool to spreading consistency. If making buttercream, beat the softened butter in a mixing bowl until creamy. Gradually add the powdered sugar and beat until light and fluffy. Add the vanilla extract or other flavoring and mix until combined.
2. **Unroll cake:** Carefully unroll the cooled sponge cake from the parchment paper.
3. **Spread filling:** Spread the prepared filling evenly over the surface of the sponge cake, leaving a small border around the edges.
4. **Roll cake:** Gently roll the filled sponge cake back up into a log shape, using the parchment paper to help lift and guide it. Place the seam side down.

For decoration:

1. **Trim ends:** Trim a small diagonal slice from each end of the rolled cake to resemble branches.
2. **Decorate with frosting:** Use a spatula to spread frosting over the surface of the rolled cake, creating a bark-like texture. Drag the tines of a fork through the frosting to create wood grain patterns.
3. **Optional decorations:** Dust the Bûche de Noël with powdered sugar to resemble snow. Decorate with chocolate shavings to mimic bark, and add meringue mushrooms or marzipan decorations for a whimsical touch.
4. **Chill:** Refrigerate the decorated Bûche de Noël for at least 1 hour to set the frosting and filling.

5. Serve: Transfer the chilled Bûche de Noël to a serving platter and slice to serve.

Bûche de Noël is a beautiful and festive dessert that's sure to impress your guests during the holiday season. Enjoy the rich flavors and charming decorations reminiscent of a cozy winter scene!

Pithiviers

Ingredients:

For the puff pastry:

- 2 sheets of ready-made puff pastry, chilled (or homemade if you prefer)

For the frangipane filling:

- 1/2 cup (115g) unsalted butter, softened
- 1/2 cup (100g) granulated sugar
- 1 cup (100g) almond flour
- 2 large eggs
- 1 teaspoon almond extract
- 1 tablespoon all-purpose flour

For assembly and decoration:

- 1 egg, beaten (for egg wash)
- Powdered sugar, for dusting (optional)

Instructions:

For the frangipane filling:

1. Prepare frangipane: In a mixing bowl, cream together the softened butter and granulated sugar until light and fluffy.
2. Add eggs: Beat in the eggs one at a time, mixing well after each addition.
3. Add almond extract and flour: Stir in the almond extract and all-purpose flour until well combined.
4. Add almond flour: Finally, fold in the almond flour until you have a smooth and creamy mixture. Set aside.

For assembly:

1. Preheat oven and prepare baking sheet: Preheat your oven to 400°F (200°C). Line a baking sheet with parchment paper.
2. Cut pastry circles: On a lightly floured surface, roll out the puff pastry sheets. Cut out two large circles of equal size, approximately 9 inches (23cm) in diameter. You can use a plate or a round cake pan as a guide.

3. **Fill pastry:** Place one of the pastry circles on the prepared baking sheet. Spoon the frangipane filling into the center of the pastry, spreading it evenly and leaving about a 1-inch (2.5cm) border around the edges.
4. **Top with second pastry circle:** Brush the border of the bottom pastry circle with a little water. Place the second pastry circle on top, pressing the edges gently to seal.
5. **Score and decorate:** Using the back of a knife, gently score a decorative pattern on the top pastry without cutting all the way through. Traditional designs include spirals or sunburst patterns. Be creative!
6. **Egg wash:** Brush the top of the pastry with the beaten egg to give it a beautiful golden color when baked.
7. **Bake:** Bake in the preheated oven for 25-30 minutes, or until the pastry is golden brown and puffed.
8. **Cool and serve:** Allow the Pithiviers to cool on a wire rack. Dust with powdered sugar if desired before serving.

Tips:

- **Variations:** You can add a layer of fruit jam or preserves on top of the frangipane for a different flavor profile. Apricot or raspberry jam works well.
- **Homemade Puff Pastry:** If you have the time and skill, making your own puff pastry can elevate the quality of the Pithiviers.

Pithiviers is a delightful pastry that showcases the richness of almond cream encased in flaky puff pastry. It's perfect for celebrations or as an elegant dessert for a special meal. Enjoy!

Gâteau Saint-Honoré

Ingredients:

For the puff pastry base:

- 1 sheet of puff pastry, chilled

For the pâte à choux:

- 1/2 cup (120ml) water
- 1/2 cup (120ml) milk
- 1/2 cup (115g) unsalted butter
- 1 tablespoon granulated sugar
- 1/2 teaspoon salt
- 1 cup (125g) all-purpose flour
- 4 large eggs

For the pastry cream:

- 2 cups (480ml) whole milk
- 1/2 cup (100g) granulated sugar
- 1 vanilla bean, split and seeds scraped (or 1 teaspoon vanilla extract)
- 4 large egg yolks
- 1/4 cup (30g) cornstarch
- 2 tablespoons (30g) unsalted butter

For the caramel:

- 1 cup (200g) granulated sugar
- 1/4 cup (60ml) water

For the whipped cream (Chantilly cream):

- 1 cup (240ml) heavy cream
- 2 tablespoons powdered sugar
- 1 teaspoon vanilla extract

Instructions:

For the puff pastry base:

1. Preheat oven and prepare baking sheet: Preheat your oven to 400°F (200°C). Line a baking sheet with parchment paper.
2. Cut and bake pastry: Roll out the puff pastry sheet and cut a 9-inch (23cm) circle. Place it on the prepared baking sheet, prick the surface with a fork, and bake for 15-20 minutes until golden brown. Let it cool completely.

For the pâte à choux:

1. Prepare choux pastry: In a medium saucepan, combine water, milk, butter, sugar, and salt. Bring to a boil over medium heat.
2. Add flour: Remove from heat and quickly stir in the flour until a dough forms. Return to the heat and cook, stirring constantly, for 2-3 minutes to dry out the dough slightly.
3. Add eggs: Transfer the dough to a mixing bowl and let it cool slightly. Add the eggs one at a time, beating well after each addition until the dough is smooth and glossy.
4. Pipe and bake choux puffs: Transfer the choux dough to a piping bag fitted with a large round tip. Pipe small choux puffs onto a baking sheet lined with parchment paper. Bake at 400°F (200°C) for 20-25 minutes until golden brown. Let cool.

For the pastry cream:

1. Heat milk: In a saucepan, heat the milk and vanilla bean (if using) until just boiling. Remove from heat and let it infuse for 10 minutes.
2. Whisk yolks and cornstarch: In a bowl, whisk together the egg yolks, sugar, and cornstarch until smooth.
3. Combine mixtures: Gradually whisk the hot milk into the egg yolk mixture. Return the mixture to the saucepan and cook over medium heat, whisking constantly, until it thickens and comes to a boil.
4. Cool pastry cream: Remove from heat, stir in the butter, and let the pastry cream cool completely. Remove the vanilla bean if used. Transfer to a piping bag.

For the caramel:

1. Prepare caramel: In a saucepan, combine the sugar and water. Cook over medium heat without stirring until the sugar dissolves and turns a golden caramel color.
2. Coat choux puffs: Dip the tops of the choux puffs into the caramel and place them on a parchment-lined sheet to set.

For the whipped cream:

1. Prepare Chantilly cream: In a mixing bowl, whip the heavy cream with powdered sugar and vanilla extract until stiff peaks form. Transfer to a piping bag fitted with a star tip.

Assembly:

1. Prepare choux ring: Pipe a ring of pâte à choux dough around the edge of the baked puff pastry circle. Bake at 400°F (200°C) for about 20 minutes until the ring is golden and puffed. Let cool.
2. Fill choux puffs: Fill the caramel-coated choux puffs with pastry cream.
3. Assemble gâteau: Arrange the filled choux puffs around the edge of the puff pastry base, attaching them with a little caramel.
4. Fill center with pastry cream: Pipe the remaining pastry cream into the center of the gâteau.
5. Decorate with Chantilly cream: Pipe rosettes of whipped cream over the top of the gâteau.
6. Final touches: Optionally, you can add extra caramel decorations or a dusting of powdered sugar.

Serving:

Refrigerate the Gâteau Saint-Honoré until ready to serve. This elegant and delicious dessert is perfect for special occasions and will impress any guest with its beautiful presentation and delightful flavors. Enjoy!

Poire Belle Hélène

Ingredients:

For the poached pears:

- 4 firm pears, such as Bosc or Bartlett
- 4 cups (1 liter) water
- 1 cup (200g) granulated sugar
- 1 vanilla bean, split and seeds scraped (or 1 teaspoon vanilla extract)
- Juice of 1 lemon

For the chocolate sauce:

- 4 ounces (115g) semi-sweet or dark chocolate, chopped
- 1/2 cup (120ml) heavy cream
- 2 tablespoons (30g) unsalted butter
- 1 tablespoon light corn syrup (optional, for shine)
- 1 teaspoon vanilla extract

For serving:

- Vanilla ice cream
- Sliced almonds, toasted (optional)

Instructions:

For the poached pears:

1. Prepare the poaching liquid: In a large saucepan, combine the water, granulated sugar, vanilla bean (or extract), and lemon juice. Bring the mixture to a boil, stirring until the sugar dissolves.
2. Prepare the pears: While the poaching liquid is heating, peel the pears, leaving the stems intact. Core the pears from the bottom using a melon baller or a small spoon to remove the seeds.
3. Poach the pears: Carefully add the peeled pears to the poaching liquid. Reduce the heat to a simmer and poach the pears for about 15-20 minutes, or until they are tender when pierced with a knife. The time will vary depending on the ripeness of the pears.

4. Cool the pears: Once the pears are tender, remove them from the poaching liquid and let them cool. You can poach the pears in advance and refrigerate them in the poaching liquid until ready to serve.

For the chocolate sauce:

1. Melt the chocolate: In a heatproof bowl, combine the chopped chocolate, heavy cream, unsalted butter, and corn syrup (if using). Set the bowl over a saucepan of simmering water (double boiler method) and stir until the chocolate is melted and the mixture is smooth.
2. Add vanilla: Remove the bowl from the heat and stir in the vanilla extract. Let the chocolate sauce cool slightly before serving.

Assembly:

1. Prepare the ice cream: Scoop the vanilla ice cream into serving bowls or plates.
2. Add the pears: Place a poached pear next to the ice cream in each bowl.
3. Drizzle with chocolate sauce: Generously drizzle the warm chocolate sauce over the pears and ice cream.
4. Garnish: If desired, sprinkle with toasted sliced almonds for an extra touch of texture and flavor.

Serving:

Serve Poire Belle Hélène immediately, allowing the contrast between the warm chocolate sauce and the cold ice cream to shine. This dessert is perfect for special occasions or as a delightful end to a meal. Enjoy the elegant simplicity and delightful combination of flavors!

Palmier

Ingredients:

- 1 sheet of puff pastry, thawed (store-bought or homemade)
- 1/2 cup (100g) granulated sugar
- 1 teaspoon ground cinnamon (optional)

Instructions:

1. Prepare the Work Surface:

    - Sprinkle about 1/4 cup of the sugar (mixed with the cinnamon, if using) evenly over your work surface.

2. Roll Out the Puff Pastry:

    - Unfold the thawed puff pastry sheet and place it on the sugared surface.
    - Sprinkle the remaining sugar evenly over the top of the pastry.
    - Roll out the pastry gently to press the sugar into it and to create an even surface, about 1/8 inch (3 mm) thick.

3. Fold the Puff Pastry:

    - Starting from one long side, fold the pastry inward, about one-third of the way to the center.
    - Fold the other long side inward to meet the first fold in the center.
    - Then fold each side again toward the center to meet each other.
    - Finally, fold one half over the other, like closing a book, to form a compact log.

4. Chill the Dough:

    - Wrap the folded pastry log in plastic wrap and chill in the refrigerator for about 30 minutes. This will make it easier to cut and help maintain its shape during baking.

5. Preheat the Oven:

    - Preheat your oven to 400°F (200°C). Line a baking sheet with parchment paper.

6. Slice and Bake:

    - Once chilled, slice the pastry log into 1/4-inch (6 mm) thick slices.

- Place the slices cut-side up on the prepared baking sheet, leaving some space between them as they will expand during baking.
- If there's any remaining sugar mixture, sprinkle it over the slices.

7. Bake:

- Bake in the preheated oven for 12-15 minutes, or until the edges are golden brown and caramelized.
- Carefully flip each palmier over using a spatula, and bake for an additional 3-5 minutes, until both sides are golden and crispy.

8. Cool and Serve:

- Remove from the oven and transfer the palmiers to a wire rack to cool completely.

Tips:

- Sugar Variations: You can use different types of sugar, such as turbinado or brown sugar, for a slightly different flavor and texture.
- Add-ins: For extra flavor, you can sprinkle finely chopped nuts, a pinch of salt, or grated citrus zest on the sugar before rolling the pastry.

Palmiers are a versatile and delightful treat, perfect for serving with tea or coffee, or as an elegant addition to any dessert platter. Enjoy!

Sablés

Ingredients:

- 1 cup (225g) unsalted butter, softened
- 2/3 cup (130g) granulated sugar
- 1 large egg yolk
- 1 teaspoon vanilla extract
- 2 cups (250g) all-purpose flour
- 1/4 teaspoon salt
- 1 egg, beaten (for egg wash)
- Turbinado sugar or granulated sugar, for sprinkling (optional)

Instructions:

1. Prepare the Dough:

    1. Cream the butter and sugar: In a large mixing bowl, beat the softened butter and granulated sugar together until light and fluffy, about 2-3 minutes using a hand mixer or stand mixer.
    2. Add the egg yolk and vanilla: Mix in the egg yolk and vanilla extract until well combined.
    3. Add the dry ingredients: In a separate bowl, whisk together the flour and salt. Gradually add the flour mixture to the butter mixture, mixing just until the dough comes together. Avoid overmixing.

2. Shape the Dough:

    1. Form the dough: Divide the dough in half. Place each half on a sheet of plastic wrap and shape into a log, about 1.5 inches (4 cm) in diameter. Wrap tightly and refrigerate for at least 1 hour, or until firm. You can also freeze the dough for 30 minutes if you're short on time.

3. Preheat the Oven:

    1. Preheat: Preheat your oven to 350°F (175°C). Line a baking sheet with parchment paper.

4. Slice and Bake:

    1. Slice the cookies: Remove the dough from the refrigerator and unwrap. Using a sharp knife, slice the dough into 1/4-inch (6 mm) thick rounds.

2. Prepare for baking: Place the rounds on the prepared baking sheet, spacing them about 1 inch (2.5 cm) apart. If desired, brush the tops with the beaten egg and sprinkle with turbinado sugar or granulated sugar for extra texture and sweetness.

5. Bake:

1. Bake the cookies: Bake in the preheated oven for 12-15 minutes, or until the edges are lightly golden. Rotate the baking sheet halfway through baking for even cooking.
2. Cool: Allow the cookies to cool on

the baking sheet for 5 minutes before transferring to a wire rack to cool completely.

Tips:

- Flavor Variations: You can add different flavorings to the dough, such as lemon zest, orange zest, or almond extract, for a unique twist.
- Chocolate-Dipped Sablés: Once the cookies are cooled, you can dip them in melted chocolate and let them set on parchment paper for an extra decadent treat.
- Storage: Store the cooled cookies in an airtight container at room temperature for up to one week.

Sablés are perfect for tea time, holiday cookie trays, or just as a delightful treat anytime. Enjoy their buttery, crumbly goodness!

Tarte Normande

Ingredients:

For the pastry:

- 1 1/4 cups (160g) all-purpose flour
- 1/4 cup (50g) granulated sugar
- 1/2 cup (115g) unsalted butter, cold and cut into small pieces
- 1 large egg yolk
- 1-2 tablespoons cold water

For the filling:

- 4-5 medium apples (such as Granny Smith or Honeycrisp), peeled, cored, and sliced
- 1/4 cup (50g) granulated sugar
- 1/2 teaspoon ground cinnamon

For the custard:

- 2 large eggs
- 1/2 cup (100g) granulated sugar
- 1/2 cup (120ml) heavy cream
- 1/4 cup (60ml) whole milk
- 1 tablespoon Calvados (apple brandy) or rum (optional)
- 1 teaspoon vanilla extract
- 1/4 cup (25g) almond flour

For the topping:

- 2 tablespoons sliced almonds
- 1 tablespoon powdered sugar, for dusting

Instructions:

1. Make the Pastry:

   1. Mix dry ingredients: In a large bowl, combine the flour and granulated sugar.
   2. Cut in butter: Add the cold butter pieces and use a pastry blender or your fingers to work the butter into the flour mixture until it resembles coarse crumbs.

    3. Add egg yolk and water: Add the egg yolk and mix until the dough starts to come together. If needed, add 1-2 tablespoons of cold water, a little at a time, until the dough forms.
    4. Chill the dough: Shape the dough into a disk, wrap it in plastic wrap, and refrigerate for at least 30 minutes.

2. Prepare the Filling:

    1. Slice the apples: Peel, core, and slice the apples thinly. Toss the apple slices with the granulated sugar and ground cinnamon in a bowl. Set aside.

3. Preheat the Oven:

    1. Preheat: Preheat your oven to 375°F (190°C).

4. Roll Out and Pre-bake the Pastry:

    1. Roll out the dough: On a lightly floured surface, roll out the chilled pastry dough to fit a 9-inch (23cm) tart pan. Press the dough into the tart pan and trim any excess.
    2. Pre-bake the crust: Prick the bottom of the crust with a fork, line it with parchment paper, and fill with pie weights or dried beans. Bake for 15 minutes, then remove the weights and parchment paper and bake for another 5 minutes until lightly golden. Let it cool slightly.

5. Make the Custard:

    1. Whisk ingredients: In a medium bowl, whisk together the eggs, granulated sugar, heavy cream, milk, Calvados (if using), and vanilla extract until smooth. Stir in the almond flour.

6. Assemble the Tart:

    1. Arrange the apples: Arrange the apple slices in a circular pattern on the pre-baked tart crust.
    2. Pour the custard: Pour the custard mixture over the apples, making sure it spreads evenly.

7. Bake the Tart:

    1. Add almonds: Sprinkle the sliced almonds over the top of the tart.
    2. Bake: Bake in the preheated oven for 30-35 minutes, or until the custard is set and the tart is golden brown.

8. Cool and Serve:

    1. Cool: Allow the tart to cool in the pan on a wire rack.
    2. Dust with powdered sugar: Just before serving, dust the tart with powdered sugar.

Tips:

- Apple Varieties: Choose firm apples that hold their shape well when baked, such as Granny Smith, Honeycrisp, or Braeburn.
- Serve: Tarte Normande is delicious served warm or at room temperature. Pair it with a dollop of whipped cream or a scoop of vanilla ice cream for an extra treat.

Enjoy making and indulging in this classic French tart that beautifully combines apples, almonds, and a creamy custard!

Beignets

Ingredients:

For the Dough:

- 3/4 cup warm water (110°F or 45°C)
- 1/4 cup granulated sugar
- 1 envelope active dry yeast (2 1/4 teaspoons)
- 1 large egg, beaten
- 1/2 cup evaporated milk
- 3 1/2 cups all-purpose flour, plus extra for dusting
- 1/2 teaspoon salt
- 2 tablespoons unsalted butter, softened
- Vegetable oil, for frying

For the Topping:

- Powdered sugar, for dusting

Instructions:

1. Prepare the Dough:

    1. Activate the yeast: In a small bowl, combine the warm water, granulated sugar, and yeast. Let it sit for about 5 minutes until it becomes foamy.
    2. Mix wet ingredients: In a large mixing bowl, combine the egg, evaporated milk, and yeast mixture.
    3. Add dry ingredients: In another bowl, whisk together the flour and salt. Gradually add the flour mixture to the wet ingredients, mixing until the dough comes together.
    4. Incorporate butter: Add the softened butter and knead the dough by hand or with a stand mixer fitted with a dough hook attachment until the dough is smooth and elastic, about 5-7 minutes.
    5. Let the dough rise: Place the dough in a greased bowl, cover with a damp cloth or plastic wrap, and let it rise in a warm place for about 1-2 hours, or until it has doubled in size.

2. Shape the Dough:

1. Roll out the dough: On a lightly floured surface, roll out the dough to about 1/4-inch thickness.
2. Cut the dough: Using a sharp knife or pizza cutter, cut the dough into 2-inch squares.

3. Fry the Beignets:

1. Heat the oil: In a deep fryer or a large, heavy-bottomed pot, heat the vegetable oil to 350°F (175°C).
2. Fry the beignets: Fry a few pieces of dough at a time, being careful not to overcrowd the pot. Fry each piece for about 2-3 minutes, turning them over halfway through, until they are golden brown and puffed.
3. Drain: Use a slotted spoon to transfer the beignets to a plate lined with paper towels to drain the excess oil.

4. Serve:

1. Dust with powdered sugar: Generously dust the warm beignets with powdered sugar. Serve immediately.

Tips:

- Serving: Beignets are best served fresh and warm. Pair them with a cup of coffee or hot chocolate for a classic New Orleans experience.
- Storage: If you have leftovers, store them in an airtight container at room temperature for up to 2 days. Reheat in a 350°F (175°C) oven for a few minutes before serving.
- Flavor Variations: You can add a bit of vanilla extract or a pinch of cinnamon to the dough for added flavor.

Enjoy making and savoring these delightful, fluffy, and sweet beignets!

Mont Blanc

Ingredients:

For the Meringue:

- 3 large egg whites
- 3/4 cup (150g) granulated sugar
- 1/4 teaspoon cream of tartar (optional)
- 1/2 teaspoon vanilla extract

For the Chestnut Purée:

- 1 1/2 cups (350g) sweetened chestnut purée (available at specialty stores or homemade)
- 2 tablespoons unsweetened cocoa powder (optional, for added depth)
- 1-2 tablespoons milk (as needed, to adjust consistency)
- 1 teaspoon vanilla extract

For the Whipped Cream:

- 1 cup (240ml) heavy whipping cream
- 2 tablespoons powdered sugar
- 1/2 teaspoon vanilla extract

Instructions:

1. Prepare the Meringue:

   1. Preheat the oven: Preheat your oven to 225°F (110°C). Line a baking sheet with parchment paper.
   2. Beat the egg whites: In a clean, dry bowl, beat the egg whites until frothy. Add the cream of tartar (if using) and continue to beat until soft peaks form.
   3. Add the sugar: Gradually add the granulated sugar, a tablespoon at a time, while continuing to beat the egg whites. Beat until the mixture is glossy and stiff peaks form. Mix in the vanilla extract.
   4. Pipe the meringue: Transfer the meringue to a piping bag fitted with a round tip. Pipe small meringue discs (about 2-3 inches in diameter) onto the prepared baking sheet.

5. Bake the meringue: Bake in the preheated oven for about 1 1/2 hours, or until the meringues are dry and crisp. Turn off the oven and let the meringues cool completely in the oven with the door slightly ajar.

2. Prepare the Chestnut Purée:

   1. Mix the purée: In a bowl, combine the sweetened chestnut purée, unsweetened cocoa powder (if using), milk (as needed to adjust consistency), and vanilla extract. The mixture should be smooth and pipeable.
   2. Transfer to piping bag: Place the chestnut purée into a piping bag fitted with a small star tip.

3. Prepare the Whipped Cream:

   1. Whip the cream: In a chilled bowl, whip the heavy cream until soft peaks form. Add the powdered sugar and vanilla extract, and continue to whip until stiff peaks form.

4. Assemble the Mont Blanc:

   1. Base layer: Place a meringue disc on each serving plate.
   2. Whipped cream: Pipe or dollop a generous amount of whipped cream onto each meringue disc.
   3. Chestnut purée: Pipe the chestnut purée over the whipped cream in a spiral or nest-like pattern to resemble a mountain peak.

Tips:

- Serving: Serve the Mont Blanc immediately after assembling for the best texture contrast between the crispy meringue, smooth chestnut purée, and fluffy whipped cream.
- Storage: Store the components separately if not serving immediately. Assemble just before serving to maintain the textures.
- Garnish: You can add a dusting of powdered sugar over the top for a snowy effect or garnish with chocolate shavings or a candied chestnut.

Enjoy making and savoring this classic and sophisticated French dessert, Mont Blanc!

Religieuse

Ingredients:

For the Choux Pastry:

- 1 cup (240ml) water
- 1/2 cup (115g) unsalted butter
- 1/2 teaspoon salt
- 1 cup (125g) all-purpose flour
- 4 large eggs

For the Pastry Cream:

- 2 cups (480ml) whole milk
- 1/2 cup (100g) granulated sugar
- 1 vanilla bean, split and scraped (or 1 teaspoon vanilla extract)
- 4 large egg yolks
- 1/4 cup (30g) cornstarch
- 2 tablespoons (30g) unsalted butter

For the Icing:

- 1 cup (120g) powdered sugar
- 2-3 tablespoons strong brewed coffee (for coffee icing) or melted chocolate (for chocolate icing)
- 1 tablespoon unsalted butter (optional, for a glossy finish)

For Assembly:

- 1/2 cup (120ml) heavy cream
- 1 tablespoon powdered sugar
- 1/2 teaspoon vanilla extract

Instructions:

1. Make the Choux Pastry:

    1. Preheat the oven: Preheat your oven to 425°F (220°C). Line a baking sheet with parchment paper.
    2. Prepare the dough: In a medium saucepan, combine the water, butter, and salt. Bring to a boil over medium heat. Add the flour all at once and stir vigorously with

a wooden spoon until the mixture forms a ball and pulls away from the sides of the pan. Remove from heat and let it cool for a few minutes.
3. Add the eggs: Add the eggs one at a time, beating well after each addition until the dough is smooth and shiny.
4. Pipe the dough: Transfer the dough to a piping bag fitted with a large round tip. Pipe 8 large rounds (about 2.5 inches in diameter) and 8 smaller rounds (about 1.5 inches in diameter) onto the prepared baking sheet.
5. Bake: Bake in the preheated oven for 10 minutes, then reduce the heat to 350°F (175°C) and bake for an additional 15-20 minutes, or until the puffs are golden brown and crisp. Allow to cool completely on a wire rack.

2. Make the Pastry Cream:

1. Heat the milk: In a medium saucepan, heat the milk and vanilla bean (if using) over medium heat until it just comes to a simmer. If using vanilla extract, add it later.
2. Mix the eggs and sugar: In a bowl, whisk together the egg yolks, granulated sugar, and cornstarch until smooth.
3. Combine and thicken: Gradually whisk the hot milk into the egg mixture, then return the mixture to the saucepan. Cook over medium heat, whisking constantly, until the mixture thickens and comes to a boil. Boil for 1-2 minutes, then remove from heat. Stir in the butter and vanilla extract (if using). Transfer to a bowl, cover with plastic wrap (pressing it directly onto the surface to prevent a skin from forming), and refrigerate until cold.

3. Make the Icing:

1. Prepare the icing: In a bowl, mix the powdered sugar with the coffee or melted chocolate until smooth. Add the butter for a glossy finish, if desired.

4. Assemble the Religieuse:

1. Fill the puffs: Transfer the pastry cream to a piping bag fitted with a small round tip. Poke a hole in the bottom of each choux puff and fill with the pastry cream.
2. Ice the puffs: Dip the tops of the filled puffs into the icing, letting any excess drip off.
3. Whip the cream: In a bowl, whip the heavy cream with the powdered sugar and vanilla extract until stiff peaks form. Transfer to a piping bag fitted with a star tip.
4. Stack and decorate: Place a small cream puff on top of a large cream puff. Pipe a ring of whipped cream around the base of the small puff to resemble a ruffled collar.

Tips:

- Consistency of dough: Ensure the choux pastry dough is smooth and shiny before piping. This ensures proper rise and hollow interior.
- Chilling: Allow the pastry cream to chill thoroughly before filling the puffs.
- Stability: To ensure the small puffs stay on top of the larger ones, you can use a little extra pastry cream as "glue."

Enjoy making and indulging in this sophisticated and delicious French pastry, the Religieuse!

Tarte Bourdaloue

Ingredients:

For the Pastry Crust:

- 1 1/4 cups (160g) all-purpose flour
- 1/4 cup (50g) granulated sugar
- 1/2 cup (115g) unsalted butter, cold and cut into small cubes
- 1 large egg yolk
- 1-2 tablespoons ice water (if needed)

For the Almond Cream Filling:

- 1 cup (100g) almond flour
- 1/2 cup (100g) granulated sugar
- 1/4 cup (60g) unsalted butter, softened
- 2 large eggs
- 1 teaspoon vanilla extract

For the Pears:

- 3-4 ripe but firm pears
- 2 cups (480ml) water
- 1 cup (200g) granulated sugar
- 1 lemon, sliced
- 1 cinnamon stick (optional)
- 1 teaspoon vanilla extract (optional)

For Assembly:

- Apricot jam or fruit preserves, for glazing (optional)
- Sliced almonds, for garnish (optional)

Instructions:

1. Prepare the Pastry Crust:

   1. Mix dry ingredients: In a large bowl, whisk together the flour and sugar.
   2. Cut in butter: Add the cold cubed butter to the flour mixture. Using a pastry cutter or your fingertips, work the butter into the flour until the mixture resembles coarse crumbs.

3. Add egg yolk: Add the egg yolk and mix until the dough comes together. If the dough is too dry, add ice water, 1 tablespoon at a time, until it comes together into a smooth ball.
4. Chill: Shape the dough into a disk, wrap it in plastic wrap, and refrigerate for at least 30 minutes.

2. Prepare the Almond Cream Filling:

1. Mix ingredients: In a medium bowl, cream together the almond flour, granulated sugar, and softened butter until light and fluffy.
2. Add eggs and vanilla: Add the eggs, one at a time, mixing well after each addition. Stir in the vanilla extract until fully incorporated.

3. Prepare the Pears:

1. Peel and core the pears: Peel the pears, cut them in half, and core them. Optionally, you can poach the pears in a syrup or simply slice them thinly for baking.
2. Poach the pears (optional): In a large saucepan, combine the water, granulated sugar, lemon slices, cinnamon stick, and vanilla extract. Bring to a simmer over medium heat. Add the pear halves and simmer for about 15-20 minutes, or until they are tender but still firm. Remove the pears from the syrup and let them cool before slicing.

4. Assemble and Bake the Tart:

1. Preheat: Preheat your oven to 375°F (190°C). Place a baking sheet in the oven to preheat as well.
2. Roll out the dough: On a lightly floured surface, roll out the chilled pastry dough into a circle large enough to fit your tart pan.
3. Line the tart pan: Gently transfer the rolled-out dough to a tart pan and press it into the bottom and sides. Trim off any excess dough.
4. Spread almond cream: Spread the almond cream evenly over the bottom of the pastry crust.
5. Arrange the pears: Arrange the poached or sliced pears over the almond cream, pressing them slightly into the filling.
6. Bake: Place the tart on the preheated baking sheet and bake for 30-35 minutes, or until the crust is golden brown and the almond cream is set.
7. Cool: Allow the tart to cool slightly before removing it from the tart pan.

5. Glaze and Garnish (optional):

1. Glaze with apricot jam: If desired, heat some apricot jam or fruit preserves in a small saucepan until melted. Brush the melted jam over the top of the warm tart for a glossy finish.
2. Garnish with sliced almonds: Sprinkle sliced almonds over the top of the tart for an extra touch of flavor and texture.

Tips:

- Choosing Pears: Use ripe but firm pears for the best texture in the tart. Bartlett, Bosc, or Anjou pears work well.
- Make Ahead: You can prepare the pastry dough, almond cream, and poached pears in advance and assemble the tart just before baking.
- Variations: Feel free to experiment with different fruits or flavorings in the almond cream, such as apricots, peaches, or spices like cardamom or nutmeg.

Serve the Tarte Bourdaloue warm or at room temperature, perhaps with a dollop of whipped cream or a scoop of vanilla ice cream. Enjoy this elegant and delicious French dessert!

Gâteau Moelleux au Chocolat

Ingredients:

- 7 oz (200g) dark chocolate (around 70% cocoa), chopped
- 1/2 cup (115g) unsalted butter, plus extra for greasing
- 3/4 cup (150g) granulated sugar
- 3 large eggs
- 1/2 cup (60g) all-purpose flour
- Pinch of salt
- Cocoa powder or powdered sugar, for dusting (optional)
- Fresh berries or whipped cream, for serving (optional)

Instructions:

1. Preheat the Oven:

    1. Preheat your oven to 350°F (175°C). Grease an 8-inch (20cm) round cake pan and line the bottom with parchment paper.

2. Melt the Chocolate and Butter:

    1. In a heatproof bowl set over a saucepan of simmering water (double boiler method), melt the chopped chocolate and butter together until smooth. Alternatively, you can melt them in the microwave in short bursts, stirring in between.

3. Prepare the Batter:

    1. In a mixing bowl, whisk together the granulated sugar and eggs until well combined.
    2. Gradually pour the melted chocolate and butter mixture into the egg mixture while whisking continuously until smooth.
    3. Sift in the flour and salt, and gently fold them into the batter until just combined. Be careful not to overmix.

4. Bake the Cake:

    1. Pour the batter into the prepared cake pan and spread it out evenly.
    2. Bake in the preheated oven for about 20-25 minutes, or until the edges are set but the center is still slightly soft and gooey. The top should form a thin crust.

3. Remove the cake from the oven and let it cool in the pan for about 10 minutes. Then, carefully transfer it to a wire rack to cool completely.

5. Serve:

   1. Once cooled, dust the top of the cake with cocoa powder or powdered sugar, if desired.
   2. Slice the cake and serve it with fresh berries or a dollop of whipped cream, if desired.

Tips:

- For best results, use good quality dark chocolate with at least 70% cocoa solids for a rich chocolate flavor.
- Be careful not to overbake the cake, as it should have a soft and slightly gooey center.
- You can customize the cake by adding nuts, chocolate chips, or a splash of liqueur to the batter.
- Leftover cake can be stored in an airtight container at room temperature for up to 2 days, or in the refrigerator for up to 5 days. Reheat individual slices in the microwave for a few seconds before serving, if desired.

Enjoy making and savoring this deliciously moist and chocolatey French cake, gâteau moelleux au chocolat!

Riz au Lait

Ingredients:

- 1/2 cup (100g) short-grain white rice (such as Arborio or pudding rice)
- 4 cups (960ml) whole milk
- 1/2 cup (100g) granulated sugar
- 1 vanilla bean or 1 teaspoon vanilla extract
- Pinch of salt
- Ground cinnamon or nutmeg, for garnish (optional)

Instructions:

1. Cook the Rice:

    1. Rinse the rice under cold water until the water runs clear. This helps remove excess starch.
    2. In a large saucepan, combine the rinsed rice and milk. If using a vanilla bean, split it lengthwise and scrape out the seeds. Add both the seeds and the pod to the saucepan.
    3. Bring the mixture to a gentle boil over medium heat, then reduce the heat to low and simmer, stirring occasionally, for about 30-40 minutes, or until the rice is tender and the mixture has thickened to a creamy consistency. Be careful not to let it boil over or stick to the bottom of the pan.
    4. Remove the vanilla bean pod, if using.

2. Sweeten and Flavor:

    1. Stir in the granulated sugar and a pinch of salt, adjusting the sweetness to your taste.
    2. If using vanilla extract instead of a vanilla bean, stir it in at this point.

3. Serve:

    1. Spoon the riz au lait into serving bowls or glasses.
    2. Serve warm, at room temperature, or chilled, according to your preference.
    3. If desired, sprinkle ground cinnamon or nutmeg on top for a finishing touch.

Tips:

- For extra flavor, you can infuse the milk with other aromatics such as cinnamon sticks, citrus zest, or a splash of rum or brandy.
- Feel free to customize your riz au lait by adding raisins, chopped nuts, or a drizzle of caramel sauce.
- Leftover rice pudding can be stored in an airtight container in the refrigerator for up to 3-4 days. Enjoy it cold or gently reheat it on the stovetop or in the microwave before serving.

Enjoy making and savoring this comforting and creamy French dessert, riz au lait!

Flan Parisien

Ingredients:

For the Pastry Crust:

1 1/4 cups (160g) all-purpose flour

1/2 cup (115g) unsalted butter, cold and cut into small cubes

1/4 cup (50g) granulated sugar

1 large egg yolk

Pinch of salt

For the Custard Filling:

2 cups (480ml) whole milk

1 cup (200g) granulated sugar

1/2 cup (60g) cornstarch

4 large eggs

2 teaspoons vanilla extract

Zest of 1 lemon (optional)

Zest of 1 orange (optional)

Instructions:

1. Prepare the Pastry Crust:

In a large mixing bowl, combine the flour, granulated sugar, and salt.

Add the cold cubed butter to the flour mixture. Using a pastry cutter or your fingertips, work the butter into the flour until the mixture resembles coarse crumbs.

Add the egg yolk and mix until the dough comes together. If the dough is too dry, add a tablespoon of cold water at a time until it forms a smooth ball.

Flatten the dough into a disk, wrap it in plastic wrap, and refrigerate for at least 30 minutes.

2. Roll out and Line the Pie Pan:

Preheat your oven to 375°F (190°C).

On a lightly floured surface, roll out the chilled pastry dough into a circle large enough to line a 9-inch (23cm) pie pan. Carefully transfer the dough to the pie pan and press it into the bottom and sides. Trim off any excess dough.

Prick the bottom of the crust with a fork and line it with parchment paper. Fill the crust with pie weights or dried beans to prevent it from puffing up during baking.

Blind bake the crust in the preheated oven for about 15 minutes. Remove the weights and parchment paper and bake for an additional 5 minutes, or until the crust is lightly golden. Remove from the oven and let it cool slightly.

3. Prepare the Custard Filling:

In a saucepan, heat the milk over medium heat until it just starts to simmer. Do not boil.

In a mixing bowl, whisk together the granulated sugar and cornstarch until well combined.

Add the eggs to the sugar-cornstarch mixture and whisk until smooth and creamy.

Slowly pour the hot milk into the egg mixture, whisking constantly to prevent curdling.

Pour the mixture back into the saucepan and cook over medium heat, stirring constantly, until it thickens to a custard consistency.

Remove the custard from the heat and stir in the vanilla extract and citrus zest, if using.

4. Assemble and Bake the Flan:

Pour the custard filling into the partially baked pastry crust, smoothing the top with a spatula.

Return the flan to the oven and bake for 25-30 minutes, or until the custard is set and the top is golden brown.

Remove the flan from the oven and let it cool completely in the pan before slicing and serving.

5. Serve:

Once cooled, slice the Flan Parisien into wedges and serve at room temperature.

Optionally, dust with powdered sugar or serve with a dollop of whipped cream or fresh berries.

Tips:

For a smoother custard, strain the custard mixture through a fine-mesh sieve before pouring it into the pastry crust.

The Flan Parisien can be stored in the refrigerator for up to 3 days. Enjoy it cold or bring it to room temperature before serving.

Enjoy making and savoring this classic French dessert, Flan Parisien!

Tarte aux Abricots

Ingredients:

For the Pastry Crust:

- 1 1/4 cups (160g) all-purpose flour
- 1/2 cup (115g) unsalted butter, cold and cut into small cubes
- 1/4 cup (50g) granulated sugar
- 1 large egg yolk
- Pinch of salt

For the Apricot Filling:

- 1 lb (450g) fresh apricots, halved and pitted
- 1/4 cup (50g) granulated sugar (adjust according to sweetness of apricots)
- 1 tablespoon cornstarch
- 1 tablespoon lemon juice
- 1 teaspoon vanilla extract

For Glaze (optional):

- 2 tablespoons apricot jam or preserves
- 1 tablespoon water

Instructions:

1. Prepare the Pastry Crust:

   1. In a large mixing bowl, combine the flour, granulated sugar, and salt.
   2. Add the cold cubed butter to the flour mixture. Using a pastry cutter or your fingertips, work the butter into the flour until the mixture resembles coarse crumbs.
   3. Add the egg yolk and mix until the dough comes together. If the dough is too dry, add a tablespoon of cold water at a time until it forms a smooth ball.
   4. Flatten the dough into a disk, wrap it in plastic wrap, and refrigerate for at least 30 minutes.

2. Roll out and Line the Tart Pan:

   1. Preheat your oven to 375°F (190°C).

2. On a lightly floured surface, roll out the chilled pastry dough into a circle large enough to line a 9-inch (23cm) tart pan with a removable bottom. Carefully transfer the dough to the tart pan and press it into the bottom and sides. Trim off any excess dough.
   3. Prick the bottom of the crust with a fork to prevent it from puffing up during baking.

3. Prepare the Apricot Filling:

   1. In a mixing bowl, combine the halved and pitted apricots with granulated sugar, cornstarch, lemon juice, and vanilla extract. Toss gently to coat the apricots evenly.

4. Assemble the Tart:

   1. Arrange the apricot halves in a circular pattern over the pastry crust, starting from the outer edge and working your way towards the center.
   2. Pour any remaining sugar mixture from the bowl over the arranged apricots.
   3. Optionally, fold the edges of the pastry crust over the apricots, creating a rustic border.

5. Bake the Tart:

   1. Place the tart pan on a baking sheet to catch any drips.
   2. Bake in the preheated oven for about 30-35 minutes, or until the crust is golden brown and the apricots are tender.
   3. Remove the tart from the oven and let it cool slightly on a wire rack.

6. Glaze (optional):

   1. In a small saucepan, heat the apricot jam or preserves with water over low heat until melted and smooth.
   2. Brush the glaze over the warm tart for a glossy finish.

7. Serve:

   1. Once cooled, slice the Tarte aux Abricots into wedges and serve at room temperature.
   2. Optionally, serve with a dollop of whipped cream or vanilla ice cream.

Tips:

- Choose ripe but firm apricots for the best flavor and texture in the tart.
- Feel free to customize the tart by adding a sprinkle of almond meal or ground nuts over the pastry crust before adding the apricot filling.
- Leftover tart can be stored in the refrigerator for up to 3 days. Enjoy it cold or bring it to room temperature before serving.

Enjoy making and savoring this deliciously fruity French dessert, Tarte aux Abricots!

Petits Pots de Crème

Ingredients:

- 2 cups (480ml) heavy cream
- 1/2 cup (100g) granulated sugar
- 4 large egg yolks
- 1 teaspoon vanilla extract
- Pinch of salt
- Fresh berries or mint leaves, for garnish (optional)

Instructions:

1. Preheat the Oven:

    1. Preheat your oven to 325°F (160°C). Place a kettle of water on the stovetop to heat for the water bath.

2. Prepare the Custard:

    1. In a saucepan, heat the heavy cream over medium heat until it just starts to simmer. Do not boil.
    2. In a separate mixing bowl, whisk together the granulated sugar, egg yolks, vanilla extract, and salt until well combined.
    3. Gradually pour the hot cream into the egg yolk mixture, whisking constantly to prevent curdling.
    4. Strain the custard through a fine-mesh sieve into a pouring jug or pitcher to remove any lumps or air bubbles.

3. Bake the Petits Pots de Crème:

    1. Arrange 4-6 ramekins or small pots in a deep baking dish or roasting pan. Place a folded kitchen towel at the bottom of the dish to prevent the ramekins from sliding.
    2. Carefully pour the custard mixture into the ramekins, filling them almost to the top.
    3. Place the baking dish with the ramekins in the preheated oven. Carefully pour hot water into the baking dish, being careful not to splash water into the ramekins, until the water reaches halfway up the sides of the ramekins.
    4. Bake for about 30-35 minutes, or until the custard is set around the edges but still slightly jiggly in the center.

5. Remove the baking dish from the oven and carefully transfer the ramekins to a wire rack to cool to room temperature.

4. Chill and Serve:

1. Once cooled to room temperature, cover each ramekin with plastic wrap and refrigerate for at least 2 hours, or until well chilled and set.
2. Before serving, you can optionally garnish each petit pot de crème with fresh berries or mint leaves for a decorative touch.

Tips:

- For extra flavor, you can infuse the cream with aromatics such as cinnamon sticks, citrus zest, or a splash of liqueur before heating.
- Be careful not to overbake the petits pots de crème, as they should be creamy and smooth in texture.
- Leftover petits pots de crème can be stored in the refrigerator for up to 3 days. Enjoy them chilled straight from the fridge.

Enjoy making and savoring this elegant and creamy French dessert, petits pots de crème!

Navettes Provençales

Ingredients:

- 2 cups (250g) all-purpose flour
- 1/2 cup (100g) granulated sugar
- 1/2 teaspoon baking powder
- Pinch of salt
- 1/4 cup (60ml) vegetable oil
- 1 large egg
- 2 tablespoons orange blossom water (or grated zest of 1 lemon)
- 1 tablespoon milk (optional)
- Powdered sugar, for dusting (optional)

Instructions:

1. Preheat the Oven:

    1. Preheat your oven to 350°F (175°C). Line a baking sheet with parchment paper or silicone baking mat.

2. Prepare the Dough:

    1. In a large mixing bowl, whisk together the flour, granulated sugar, baking powder, and salt.
    2. Make a well in the center of the dry ingredients and add the vegetable oil, egg, and orange blossom water (or lemon zest).
    3. Use a fork or your hands to mix the wet and dry ingredients together until a dough forms. If the dough is too dry, add a tablespoon of milk at a time until it comes together into a smooth ball.

3. Shape the Navettes:

    1. Divide the dough into smaller portions and roll each portion into a rope about 1/2 inch (1.5cm) in diameter.
    2. Cut the ropes into pieces about 3 inches (7.5cm) long.
    3. Flatten each piece slightly with your fingers and shape the ends to resemble boat tips.

4. Bake the Navettes:

1. Place the shaped navettes on the prepared baking sheet, spacing them slightly apart.
2. Bake in the preheated oven for 12-15 minutes, or until the cookies are lightly golden brown around the edges.
3. Remove from the oven and transfer the navettes to a wire rack to cool completely.

5. Optional Dusting:

1. Once cooled, you can dust the navettes with powdered sugar for a decorative touch.

Tips:

- Be careful not to overwork the dough to avoid tough cookies. Mix until just combined.
- If you prefer a stronger citrus flavor, you can use both orange blossom water and lemon zest.
- Navettes Provençales are traditionally served during certain holidays, especially Candlemas (La Chandeleur) on February 2nd. They are also popular as a treat during Easter.

Enjoy making and savoring these delightful Navettes Provençales, redolent with the flavors of the Provence region of France!

Pain Perdu

Ingredients:

- 4 slices of day-old bread (such as French bread, brioche, or challah)
- 2 large eggs
- 1/2 cup (120ml) milk
- 1 tablespoon granulated sugar (optional, adjust to taste)
- 1 teaspoon vanilla extract or ground cinnamon (optional)
- Pinch of salt
- Butter or neutral oil, for frying
- Maple syrup, honey, or powdered sugar, for serving (optional)

Instructions:

1. Prepare the Bread:

    1. If your bread is fresh, leave it out on the counter for a few hours or overnight to stale slightly. Stale bread absorbs the egg mixture better without becoming soggy.
    2. Slice the bread into thick slices, about 1/2 to 3/4 inch (1.5 to 2 cm) thick.

2. Make the Egg Mixture:

    1. In a shallow dish or bowl, whisk together the eggs, milk, sugar (if using), vanilla extract or ground cinnamon (if using), and a pinch of salt until well combined.

3. Soak the Bread:

    1. Dip each slice of bread into the egg mixture, turning to coat both sides evenly. Allow the bread to soak for about 30 seconds on each side, ensuring it absorbs the mixture without becoming too soggy.

4. Cook the Pain Perdu:

    1. Heat a large skillet or griddle over medium heat. Add a knob of butter or a drizzle of neutral oil to the pan and swirl to coat.
    2. Once the butter is melted and the pan is hot, add the soaked bread slices in a single layer, making sure not to overcrowd the pan.
    3. Cook the pain perdu for 2-3 minutes on each side, or until golden brown and crispy on the outside and cooked through on the inside. You may need to adjust the heat if the bread is browning too quickly.

4. Transfer the cooked pain perdu to a plate and keep warm while you cook the remaining slices.

5. Serve:

   1. Serve the pain perdu warm, drizzled with maple syrup, honey, or sprinkled with powdered sugar, if desired.
   2. Garnish with fresh berries, sliced fruit, or a dollop of whipped cream for an extra touch of indulgence.

Tips:

- Feel free to customize your pain perdu by adding flavorings such as ground nutmeg, almond extract, or orange zest to the egg mixture.
- For a richer version, you can use half-and-half or heavy cream instead of milk.
- Leftover pain perdu can be stored in the refrigerator for up to 2 days. Reheat in a toaster or oven until warmed through before serving.

Enjoy making and savoring this classic French comfort food, pain perdu!

Charlotte aux Fraises

Ingredients:

For the Strawberry Mousse:

- 2 cups (300g) fresh strawberries, hulled and sliced
- 1/2 cup (100g) granulated sugar
- 2 tablespoons water
- 1 tablespoon lemon juice
- 2 teaspoons powdered gelatin
- 1/4 cup (60ml) cold water
- 1 cup (240ml) heavy cream, chilled

For the Charlotte:

- 24-30 ladyfingers (biscuits à la cuillère) or slices of sponge cake
- Additional fresh strawberries, sliced, for garnish (optional)
- Confectioners' sugar, for dusting (optional)

Instructions:

1. Prepare the Strawberry Puree:

    1. In a blender or food processor, puree the fresh strawberries until smooth.
    2. In a small saucepan, combine the strawberry puree, granulated sugar, 2 tablespoons of water, and lemon juice. Heat over medium heat, stirring occasionally, until the sugar is dissolved and the mixture is slightly thickened. Remove from heat and set aside to cool slightly.

2. Bloom the Gelatin:

    1. In a small bowl, sprinkle the powdered gelatin over 1/4 cup of cold water. Let it sit for 5-10 minutes to bloom.

3. Make the Strawberry Mousse:

    1. Once the gelatin is bloomed, microwave it for about 10-15 seconds or until fully dissolved. Allow it to cool slightly.
    2. In a mixing bowl, whip the chilled heavy cream until stiff peaks form.
    3. Gently fold the cooled gelatin mixture into the whipped cream until well combined.

4. Fold in the cooled strawberry puree until the mixture is smooth and evenly combined.

4. Assemble the Charlotte:

   1. Line the bottom and sides of a round springform pan or Charlotte mold with plastic wrap, leaving some overhang for easy removal later.
   2. Arrange the ladyfingers or sponge cake slices along the bottom and sides of the pan, pressing them gently to fit snugly together.
   3. Pour half of the strawberry mousse over the ladyfingers, spreading it out evenly with a spatula.
   4. Add another layer of ladyfingers or sponge cake slices on top of the mousse, followed by the remaining mousse.
   5. Smooth the top with a spatula and cover the Charlotte with plastic wrap.
   6. Refrigerate for at least 4 hours, or until the mousse is set.

5. Serve:

   1. Once set, carefully remove the Charlotte from the mold by lifting it out using the overhanging plastic wrap.
   2. Garnish the top with additional sliced strawberries, if desired, and dust with confectioners' sugar.
   3. Slice and serve chilled.

Tips:

- You can customize the Charlotte by adding other fruits or berries to the mousse or using a combination of different berries.
- For a more intense strawberry flavor, you can add a few drops of strawberry extract or liqueur to the mousse mixture.
- Leftover Charlotte aux Fraises can be stored in the refrigerator for up to 2 days.

Enjoy making and savoring this elegant and refreshing French dessert, Charlotte aux Fraises!

Croissant Bread Pudding

Ingredients:

- 4 large croissants, preferably stale or day-old, cut into cubes
- 2 cups (480ml) whole milk
- 1 cup (240ml) heavy cream
- 4 large eggs
- 1/2 cup (100g) granulated sugar
- 1 teaspoon vanilla extract
- Pinch of salt
- 1/2 cup (75g) raisins or chocolate chips (optional)
- Butter, for greasing the baking dish
- Powdered sugar, for dusting (optional)
- Maple syrup, caramel sauce, or whipped cream, for serving (optional)

Instructions:

1. Preheat the Oven:

    1. Preheat your oven to 350°F (175°C). Grease a baking dish with butter.

2. Prepare the Croissants:

    1. Cut the croissants into cubes and place them in the prepared baking dish. If the croissants are fresh, you can toast them in the oven for a few minutes to dry them out slightly.

3. Make the Custard Mixture:

    1. In a mixing bowl, whisk together the whole milk, heavy cream, eggs, granulated sugar, vanilla extract, and a pinch of salt until well combined.
    2. If using, stir in the raisins or chocolate chips.

4. Pour the Custard Over the Croissants:

    1. Pour the custard mixture over the croissant cubes, making sure all the croissants are evenly soaked. Press down gently to submerge the croissants if needed.
    2. Let the croissants soak in the custard mixture for about 15-20 minutes, allowing them to absorb the liquid.

5. Bake the Bread Pudding:

1. Place the baking dish in the preheated oven and bake for 40-45 minutes, or until the bread pudding is set and golden brown on top.
2. If the top starts to brown too quickly, you can cover the baking dish with aluminum foil halfway through baking.

6. Serve:

1. Once baked, remove the croissant bread pudding from the oven and let it cool for a few minutes.
2. Dust with powdered sugar, if desired, before serving.
3. Serve warm with maple syrup, caramel sauce, whipped cream, or your favorite topping.

Tips:

- You can customize your croissant bread pudding by adding other ingredients such as sliced bananas, chopped nuts, or a splash of rum or bourbon to the custard mixture.
- Leftover croissant bread pudding can be stored in the refrigerator for up to 3 days. Reheat individual portions in the microwave or oven before serving.

Enjoy making and savoring this decadent and comforting croissant bread pudding!

www.ingramcontent.com/pod-product-compliance
Lightning Source LLC
LaVergne TN
LVHW081556060526
838201LV00054B/1913